Parliaments and Legislatures

Janet M. Box-Steffensmeier and David T. Canon, Series Editors

Authorizing Policy

Thad Hall

The Ohio State University Press
Columbus

328.73076
H17a

Library of Congress Cataloging-in-Publication Data
M/C

Hall, Thad E.
  Authorizing policy / Thad Hall.
    p. cm. — (Parliaments and legislatures series)
  Includes bibliographical references and index.
  ISBN 0-8142-0972-6 (cloth : alk. paper) — ISBN 0-8142-9042-6 (CD)
1. Budget process—United States. 2. Budget—United States. 3. United
States. Congress—Committees. 4. Government spending—United
States—Decision making. 5. United States—Appropriations and expen-
ditures—Decision making. 6. Policy sciences. I. Title. II. Series.
  HJ2051.H335 2004
  328.73'07657—dc22
                          2004008804

Cover design by Dan O'Dair.
Type set in Minion.
Printed by Thomson-Shore, Inc.

The paper used in this publication meets the minimum requirements of
the American National Standard for Information Sciences—Permanence of
Paper for Printed Library Materials. ANSI Z39.48–1992.

9 8 7 6 5 4 3 2 1

Contents

List of Figures

List of Tables

Acknowledgments

This book brings together two halves of my life—the academic who is interested in puzzles about American politics and the person who has worked in the policy world in Washington, D.C. In fact, this book comes directly from a decision I made in February 1996 to leave the Ph.D. program at the University of Georgia to move to Washington, D.C., to take a position as a policy analyst for the Southern Governors' Association. Soon after taking the job, I found myself listed in the *Washington Representatives* and educating members of Congress on the reauthorization of the federal surface transportation program. During this process, I noticed how key players in this process had been quietly gearing up for the reauthorization for two years, determining how to win the fight in order to make the policy work better for them. I also saw how my friends were all bored stiff the year after the authorization ended. This observation led to my interest in how short-term authorizations control the process of policy change.

I therefore have two sets of people to thank. Inside the beltway, Doug Callaway of the Florida Department of Transportation taught me everything I know about surface transportation and about how the reauthorization process works in the real world. Many other lobbyists—including Becky Weber, Geoff Trego, David Soilou, Lydia Conrad, Debbie Marshall, and Dawn Levy—helped to round out my Washington education. I am also most indebted to Elizabeth Schneider, executive director of the Southern Governors' Association, for the trust she placed in my ability to work on transportation policy, which is the single largest federal policy on which the governors lobbied during my tenure at SGA.

In the academic world, I am indebted to Scott Ainsworth, who provided a tremendous amount of support as both a friend and colleague as I worked on this project. Scott Adler read my initial dissertation and made very helpful recommendations about how to rewrite it as a book. He also recommended the book to The Ohio State University Press. David King provided me with a very thorough review of the book and helped me at various points in the process to improve the analysis. Bryan Jones and John Wilkerson both made helpful comments to me throughout this process and provided encouraging thoughts about how to make it better. Mike Alvarez, Tom Lauth, Larry O'Toole, Arnie Fleischmann, and Hal Rainey also provided insightful comments that improved this book. Finally, Malcolm Litchfield at The Ohio State University Press was very helpful in moving this manuscript through the process and also illuminated for me the link between diet books and writing political science, for which I am very grateful.

Finally, I must acknowledge the torture that I put my wife through in writing this book. She has read the entire document multiple times, ensuring that she is the only health care lawyer in America who understands short-term authorizations. She endured my working on this project on weekends and after work, and was incredibly supportive throughout this project. I dedicate this book to her.

1

Policy Periodicity

Lawmaking is typically seen through the lens of pressure politics, partisan politics, and contingencies. Policies pass or fail because of interest groups' activities, manipulations by political parties, or because legislators are playing catch-up in the aftermath of a traumatic event, such as September 11th. This type of legislative activity often gets a large amount of coverage and attention, and to the casual observer, most legislative activity may seem to happen this way. Much like ESPN Sports Center—which highlights the slam dunks, home runs, and spectacular football plays—the political media and political scientists often cover lawmaking in the same way, emphasizing the big events.

And of course, sometimes Congress does work this way,[1] yet there are also many regular and predictable cycles in the legislative process, such as elections and budgets and appropriations. This book explores the least understood of these cycles: the strategic use of short-term authorizations. Large parts of the domestic and international policy agenda appear on the legislative agenda at regularized intervals. The annual defense authorization is an obvious case in point, but any legislation with a short-term authorization—that is, a funding authorization or actual policy authorization that is for only a limited time—will necessarily return to the legislative agenda to be reauthorized.

Scholars have been studying aspects of reauthorizations—the term used for the renewal of a short-term authorization—for some time. Anyone who has examined the distribution of transportation projects (e.g., Evans 1994), regulatory policy (e.g., Baumgartner and Jones 1993), education policy (e.g., Chubb 1985), or defense policy (e.g., Art 1985, 1989) in the last twenty to thirty years has studied a reauthorization. From this, we have learned much about the dynamics that dominate single reauthorizations. However, we know little from systematic study about how or why Congress uses this procedure, which brings issues again and again back on the congressional radar.

This book is about something very simple yet very important for understanding how Congress works—and how policy is made in Washington—year in and year out. It is about how Congress controls the timing of policy change and how it builds into many of the laws it passes a simple mechanism for ensuring that the specific policy that the law covers will be revisited by Congress at a future point in time. It is about short-term authorizations and program reauthorizations. Short-term authorizations vary in their length, form, and function. In this book, I examine these variations and consider how their use can help explain a variety of behaviors in Congress, from the timing of legislative action to the forms of oversight committees undertake.

Studying short-term authorizations is not some theoretical exercise, a model of a hypothetical event that is interesting only because it occurs occasionally. Short-term authorizations drive Congress; just ask President George W. Bush's Senior White House Adviser Karl Rove.

> Now comes word that [Karl] Rove [senior adviser to President Bush] . . .
> has asked all of the Cabinet agencies for lists of any legislation that will
> expire before Bush's term ends in January 2005. . . . Rove's request is an
> effort, as a White House official said, to see "what issues might be driving
> the congressional agenda" in the future—and by extension, Bush's politi-
> cal prospects in November 2004 (Milbank 2002).

Many key reasons for studying short-term authorizations can be found in this excerpt. Their use covers the policy landscape—few cabinet departments or regulatory agencies escape having some programs covered by short-term authorizations. They drive the congressional agenda. They affect the political prospects of the White House and members of Congress, who are able to shape policy debates, the distribution of benefits, and the way in which the federal government—and all policy actors who touch the federal government—operates into the future. And, until now, no one has focused on how this simple feature of the legislative process drives the policy debate on both ends of Pennsylvania Avenue.

Consider the following case, which highlights the dominance of short-term authorizations on the legislative landscape.

Education Reform 2001: Where's "Head Start"?

During the 2000 presidential campaign, President George Bush pledged to reform the nation's elementary and secondary education programs. One component of his reform agenda was to dramatically change the federal

Head Start program, which primarily serves the nation's low-income three- and four-year-olds. During the campaign, Bush proposed moving Head Start from the Department of Health and Human Services to the Department of Education. He also wanted the early education program to change its focus as well, with a greater emphasis on reading and results measured through testing. When he was president-elect, Bush met with senior congressional leaders to discuss educational issues; his Head Start proposal was one of the items on the agenda.

After his inauguration, President Bush made his first week in office "Education Week," and the Thursday stop on his education tour was a visit to a Head Start program. In keeping with the theme of the importance of education to the new president, the first legislative initiative he sent to Capitol Hill was his No Child Left Behind education proposal. This proposal captured the president's goals for reforming elementary and secondary education, with its focus on standards and accountability. However, the legislative proposal the president sent to Congress was missing one thing: his proposed reforms for the Head Start program. The legislation was the centerpiece of President Bush's education reform agenda, but despite the importance of this legislation, Head Start reform was not there.

The answer to why it was not there was simple. As *The New York Times* reported on February 10, 2001, "Mr. Bush's aides said this week that they would not seek to move Head Start until the program is eligible for reauthorization by Congress, in 2003" (Steinberg 2001). The reason that the administration did not include the transfer of Head Start to the Department of Education in the largest, most important education bill considered by Congress during the president's first term was that the short-term authorization governing the Head Start program had not expired; it was not up for reauthorization. Therefore, changing Head Start was not on the table.

A New Understanding of Short-Term Authorizations

Short-term authorizations serve as a critical tool for controlling policy change by channeling it into a specific time point—when an authorization expires. With a short-term authorization, Congress and its committees can gain the benefits that accrue from planning when legislative activity will occur and ensuring that a given policy issue is taken off of the legislative agenda for a fixed period of time between authorizations. Short-term authorizations induce stability by serving as a gatekeeping mechanism, insulating committees from the pressure to revise public policy constantly for stakeholders who lost in the last legislative battle and providing a fixed point at which the status quo will be reconsidered.

The benefits of induced stability are well illustrated in the case of surface transportation policy, which is currently reauthorized on a six-year cycle. During each reauthorization, the legislation is recrafted—the funding formulas, the "high priority projects," and the specific regulations and requirements—to benefit individual members. The distribution of these benefits assists members in their efforts to achieve reelection and to accomplish institutional goals (Fenno 1973; Mayhew 1974). Additionally, by distributing these projects with some regularity (roughly twice a decade), the committee can build winning policy coalitions (e.g., Evans 1994) and increase the influence of committee members by determining which members get projects. The difficulty of crafting these deals, and the lack of will to do so between authorizations, is well described by a person who has been a player in three surface transportation authorizations:

> The committee does not move between authorizations because there is no "have to" without a funding expiration or something similar. Even with a trigger [to end the flow of funds to states if an authorization is not completed], funding to states has lapsed in the last two authorizations. People just can't bear to go through the process more than once every six years. Hell, we can't even get technical corrections bills passed. The 1991 bill was written in the middle of the night and riddled with errors, but there was no way to fix it. We finally fixed it when we did the NHS [legislation creating the National Highway System], and it only passed because of the money trigger that it had.[2]

Once all of the deals have been struck and the benefits have been distributed, members have an incentive for surface transportation policy to be taken off the legislative agenda so that their deals do not unravel (e.g., Lee 1998, 2003). For example, a senator who agreed to support the bill because it contains several high profile highway projects for her state but at the cost of lower overall revenues for her state from the transportation funding formulas can have confidence that the legislation will remain in place for the entire authorized period and that she will receive all of the projects she is promised in the authorization. Also, postponing action in a policy area to the next reauthorization keeps legislation in that area from moving to the floor whenever there is an atypical number of legislative or nonlegislative hearings, a raised level of media coverage of an issue, or new information that changed some aspect of the general understanding of the issue. Without this predictability, crafting legislation could be difficult because members whose previous deals would be undone would likely protest.

Short-term authorizations also help Congress address the problem of scheduling by developing an operational agenda (e.g., Loomis 1994). Everyone knows when a given program will be reconsidered.

It is also clear that short-term authorizations profoundly influence the policy environment in the following ways. First, short-term authorizations play an important role in the ability of members to achieve their goals. It is well understood that Congress is organized to promote the reelection of members. Members may have other interests, but "the goal [of being reelected] must be achieved over and over if other ends are to be entertained" (Mayhew 1974, 16). The committee system provides members with a forum in which to engage in advertising, credit claiming, and position taking, activities that are essential to a member's quest for reelection. Other scholars (Ferejohn 1974; Fiorina 1977) suggest that a member's reelection interests are best achieved through other activities—such as lawmaking, pork barreling, and casework—and some are kind enough to suggest that some politicians even want to make good public policy (e.g., Fenno 1973).

Short-term authorizations create opportunities for members to engage in all of these forms of reelection activities. When a program is up for reauthorization, members can claim credit for past program successes, take positions on existing policies and new initiatives, advocate for new initiatives—including important projects for their district—and advertise their views. A reauthorization often leads to actual lawmaking, affording members the opportunity to claim credit for accomplishing something on an important issue. Some members make trades in legislation that bring benefits to their district, while others make important policy contributions. One example of this is the reauthorization of surface transportation programs, which now occurs on a six-year time frame. With the transportation reauthorization, members can push for better highway or transit funding formulas for their state, apply for a "high priority" project for their district, claim credit for past program successes, and then claim credit for the benefits the bill will provide their district—in jobs and better transportation—once the legislation is completed.

Second, short-term authorizations explain certain congressional committee behavior and augment our understanding of committees. For example, Krehbiel (1991) argues that committees are designed to encourage members to gain expertise. Short-term authorizations can be understood as being a procedure designed to ensure that the expertise of members is kept current—by bringing an issue before its members at regular intervals—and that their expertise is used to improve existing policies. Committees can also give a program an authorization length that allows information to be used immediately or to be collected with other data on the issue and used in the future. For example, defense policy is reauthorized annually, allowing committees to put information to use immediately. By contrast, elementary and secondary education policy is reauthorized every six years, which allows committees to collect information about education policy over time and then incorporate all of this information at the appropriate time.

Similarly, distributive theories of Congress note that legislators desire to capture gains from logrolling and trades and will create rules and institutions that ensure this occurs (e.g., Evans 1994, Ferejohn 1974; Shepsle 1978; and Weingast and Marshall 1988). Short-term authorizations can easily be seen as a mechanism for facilitating trades by ensuring that (*a*) legislative vehicles for trade emerge from a committee at given times; (*b*) trades made will be in place for a fixed period and members will not have to continually renegotiate trades; and (*c*) future opportunities will exist to punish those who cheat and do not uphold their end of the trade.

This point can again be illustrated by using surface transportation as an example. The surface transportation bill is a cornucopia for members in that it typically authorizes not just funding for ongoing highway and transit programs, but also more than a thousand individual earmarks—special funding for projects of the members' choosing. Every six years, there is a bill for these transportation programs and projects, and over the life of the bill, the specific benefit that a member requested can be provided. Because the bill lasts for six years, a member can rest assured that the project they requested in exchange for their vote—and some members are actually making a direct trade-off between receiving more projects versus high overall highway and transit funding for their community—will be carried out. Likewise, members who cheat—like Budget Committee members who receive projects but then do not support high levels of transportation funding—can be punished in the future.

Third, short-term authorizations change the dynamic of studying how policies change over time. Many scholars, including Kingdon (1995), Baumgartner and Jones (1993), and Sabatier and Jenkins-Smith (1993), have examined the role played by the media, interest groups, and other stakeholders in bringing issues onto the government agenda, in terms of how these issues are framed and reframed and what level of policy change is likely to occur. However, while these studies are well crafted to identify the level of change that may occur and in what direction the policy may change—for example, more regulatory or more libertarian—they are not designed to identify when policy change will occur. As I will demonstrate in later chapters, there is an important role played by short-term authorizations in the process determining the timing of policy change. For those programs with a short-term authorization, the expiration of an authorization likely determines the time when Congress will act on an issue. Those stakeholders who have an interest in changing a policy are well served to ensure that their actions are timed to coincide with the reauthorization schedule of the program in which they are interested.

Fourth, the induced stability that arises from the use of short-term authorizations—and the revisiting of program management and design issues that occur during reauthorizations—affects the implementation process. Implementation requires public managers to have the ability to manage networks of actors with a given set of instruments and resources (e.g., O'Toole 1997; Pressman and Wildavsky 1984). Although managers have—to a greater or lesser extent—discretion over how to implement a policy, certain factors constrain them. The laws creating a program are often quite detailed, stating which actors must be involved in the imple-mentation and the tools and structures that have to be used to achieve these goals (e.g., Hall and O'Toole 2000, 2004). The reauthorization process allows implementers to present to Congress their concerns and to attempt to change the existing law so that the implementation of the pro-gram in question can be made more effective and efficient. This process in many ways mirrors Lasswell's (1956) stages of the policy decision process, with groups engaging in implementation and evaluation after the law is passed, and then using these data and experience as they engage in policy analysis that can feed into the next reauthorization.

Fifth, this study expands our understanding of short-term authorizations that come from studies of oversight or from studies of appropriations and budgeting. Scholars of congressional oversight of the executive have argued that the regularity of review that comes from short-term authorizations facilitates oversight (e.g., Aberbach 1991; Fisher 1983, 1979; Oleszek 1989; Schick 1995, 1980; Shuman 1992; Tiefer 1989). The theory goes that when the authorization of a program is to expire, Congress holds hearings in order to determine how effectively the program has functioned. Aberbach (1991) found that members of authorization committees rank the expiration of an authorization as being a key reason why committee oversight occurs. Scholars of budgeting and appropriations argue that short-term authoriza-tions are designed to give authorizing committees greater control over the funding a policy receives vis-à-vis the Appropriations Committee (e.g., Fenno 1966; Ippolito 1981; Schick 1995; Shuman 1992; Wildavsky 1992). Many short-term authorizations contain funding targets for how much money should be appropriated for the program in order for it to function optimally. This allows authorizers to signal to appropriators, and relevant interest groups, a preferred program funding level.

While the claims made in the previous paragraph have some merit—both are tested in later chapters with mixed results—I argue that they are not the most important reasons for the use of short-term authorizations. In the analysis that follows, I will show that short-term authorizations are important to committees because they are an effective tool for controlling when policy action occurs in a committee. Controlling the timing of policy change, in turn, creates policy stability. Congressional committees face tremendous pressure from groups, constituents, and even their colleagues to address certain issues; short-term authorizations function as a framework within which these policies can be acted upon in a structured manner.

Plan of the Book

In chapter 2, I explain the use and function of short-term authorizations. This discussion focuses on how short-term authorizations fit into the rules of the House and Senate. Additionally, I discuss the 1959 Russell Amendment, which used a short-term authorization as a tool for improving policy analysis within the legislative branch related to defense procurement policy.

In chapter 3 there is a detailed articulation of the thesis of the book—that short-term authorizations serve as a mechanism for controlling the timing of policy change—which is defined as a change in the law underlying a program or agency. I discuss how this mechanism allows Congress to control its own agenda, create a stable policy environment, and ensure that previous agreements made by members regarding the enactment and implementation of a given law are completed before these agreements are reconsidered.

Chapter 4 examines the impact of short-term authorizations on the appropriations process. Some scholars have argued that the funding levels included in many short-term authorizations are designed to serve as a signaling mechanism from authorizers to appropriators. Analyzing how Congress treats programs with various authorization types over time, I find that the signaling effect of authorized funding levels declined dramatically from fiscal year 1977 to 1998, especially after strict rules over appropriations were adopted as part of the Budget Enforcement Act.

Chapter 5 is the first of two chapters that consider how short-term authorizations facilitate oversight. The analysis in this chapter focuses on whether the expiration of an authorization encourages Congress to hold hearings. The analysis finds that Congress is rather diligent in holding oversight hearings during the life span of a given program authorization. With the exception of one case, there is not a significant spike in hearing activity when a program expires.

This discussion of oversight continues in chapter 6 with a consideration of the oversight that arises when Congress acts through the legislative process to modify the way in which programs operate. Using case studies of the Head Start program, the mass transit program, and the Commodity Futures Trading Commission, I show that reauthorizations are typically major events in the life of a program, offering Congress an opportunity to make significant modifications to a given program.

The main hypothesis of the book—that the expiration of an authorization is the critical point at which policy change occurs—is tested in chapter 7. The data show that the expiration of an authorization as the primary point at which the law governing a given program or policy—such as mass transit—changes. Other factors that have been touted as important to the process of policy change—such as hearings and media coverage—may change people's perceptions of an issue, but they are not critical in opening up the legislative process so that changes in the law can occur.

Chapter 8 examines trends related to short-term authorizations during the 1990s. The number of programs operating with expired authorizations more than doubled from 1993 to 1994, and there has been little change in the situation since. As a result, an increasing number of programs operate without the effective oversight of authorizing committees. This creates a situation where authorizers no longer have effective control over programs under their jurisdiction and agencies are unable to get needed modifications to the laws governing their operations.

In the final chapter, I review the findings of the empirical analyses that support the importance of short-term authorizations as a mechanism for controlling policy change. Building on this point, I consider the possible benefits that may accrue to Congress more broadly through the use of short-term authorizations, especially related to the control of the congressional schedule. I also consider the potential implications of short-term authorizations on the people who actually have to implement laws once Congress passes the new law. Finally, I close with an examination of how short-term authorizations fit into normative theories of the democratic process.

Finally, there is a Methodological Appendix, which explains the research design used to analyze short-term authorizations. The analysis combines the benefits of examining specific policies over a long period of time with those that come from examining multiple programs across several policy areas and congressional committees. Three policy areas—education, transportation, and regulatory policy—are the focus of this study, with other policy areas, especially defense, also used to make specific points about the authorization process.

2

How Short-Term Authorizations Work

In 1965, Congress created the Appalachian Regional Commission. Among other things, this legislation authorized the creation of the commission by stating in section 101 that:

> (a) There is hereby established an Appalachian Regional Commission. . . .
> In carrying out the purposes of this Act, the Commission shall . . . develop
> . . . comprehensive and coordinated plans and programs.[1]

The act also contained the following section, which served to make the authorization short-term:

> Sec. 401. In addition to the appropriations authorized in section 201 for
> the Appalachian development highway system, there is hereby authorized
> to be appropriated for the period ended June 30, 1967, to be available
> until expended, not to exceed $252,400,000 to carry out this Act.[2]

This example illustrates three general features of authorization legislation in the post–World War II era. First, there is a substantive component that establishes a program and structures its operations so that the program will be implemented in the manner that the committee desires (Oleszek 1989; Schick 1995; Tiefer 1989). Second, authorizing legislation has a fiscal component that authorizes the appropriation of funds. This signals to appropriators and to other policy stakeholders the funding levels that the authorizing committee thinks are appropriate for the program. Third, the authorization may be limited in time, thus short-term in nature. The idea of control is the basis for these components of an authorization. The committee wants to control how a program operates, influence how much money is spent to make this happen, and identify the time at which the program should be reconsidered by Congress. Committees make an authorization short-term to attempt to achieve control over the program on an ongoing basis.

The Rules: How They Work and How to Break Them

The use of short-term authorizations is rule-based; it leverages House and Senate rules prohibiting unauthorized appropriations that were adopted in the mid-1800s. House rule XXI, clause 2, k and Senate rule XVI both state that (*a*) no appropriation shall be made for a program that does not have an authorization, and (*b*) no appropriation bill shall make changes to existing law (Schick 1995; Tiefer 1989). Short-term authorizations leverage this rule by making a portion of the authorization, typically the authorization of appropriations, temporary.

The language that was adopted by the House and Senate in the mid-1800s prohibiting unauthorized appropriations has been retained, with only slight modification, to this date, as tables 2.1 and 2.2 show (Schick 1995; Tiefer 1989). Although the Senate rules on unauthorized appropriations are more lenient than the rules of the House, both chambers have, for more than 150 years, attempted to limit substantially unauthorized appropriations, except in the case of continuing expenditures for public work projects and other capital projects for which construction is already in progress (Schick 1995).

The rules themselves contain exceptions that allow unauthorized appropriations to occur (Schick 1995; Tiefer 1989). Continuing resolutions, which provide interim funding in cases where regular appropriations bills do not pass, are not covered by the prohibition against unauthorized appropriations. There are also procedures for waiving the rules entirely. In the House, the Rules Committee can assign appropriations bills a special rule that waives the point of order on unauthorized appropriations. In some years, the percentage of the nondefense discretionary appropriations that are for unauthorized programs can be quite high (Meyers 1988). The rule can cover all or a limited number of unauthorized appropriations in a bill. For example, on July 24, 1991, the House of Representatives considered the Department of Transportation and Related Agencies Appropriations Act. The rule for this bill—House Resolution 200—read, in part:

> Resolved, That during the consideration of the bill (H.R. 2942) making appropriations for the Department of Transportation and related agencies . . . all points of order against provisions in the bill for failure to comply with the provisions of clauses 2 and 6 of rule XXI are hereby waived. It shall be in order to consider the amendments printed in the report of the Committee on Rules accompanying this resolution, if offered by the Member specified or his designee, and all points of order against the amendments for failure to comply with the provisions of clause 7 of rule XVI and clause 2 of rule XXI are hereby waived.[3]

Table 2.1 The Rules of the Senate Governing Expired Authorizations

---

Standing Rules of The Senate

Rule XVI: Appropriations and Amendments to General Appropriations Bills

1. On a point of order made by any Senator, no amendments shall be received to any general appropriation bill the effect of which will be to increase an appropriation already contained in the bill, or to add a new item of appropriation, unless it be made to carry out the provisions of some existing law . . . or unless the same be moved by direction of the Committee on Appropriations or of a committee of the Senate having legislative jurisdiction of the subject matter . . .

2. The Committee on Appropriations shall not report an appropriation bill containing amendments to such bill proposing new or general legislation or any restriction on the expenditure of the funds appropriated which proposes a limitation not authorized by law if such restriction is to take effect or cease to be effective upon the happening of a contingency, and if an appropriation bill is reported to the Senate containing amendments to such bill proposing new or general legislation or any such restriction, a point of order may be made against the bill, and if the point is sustained, the bill shall be recommitted to the Committee on Appropriations.[. . .]

4. On a point of order made by any Senator, no amendment offered by any other Senator which proposes general legislation shall be received to any general appropriation bill, nor shall any amendment not germane or relevant to the subject matter contained in the bill be received; nor shall any amendment to any item or clause of such bill be received which does not directly relate thereto; nor shall any restriction on the expenditure of the funds appropriated which proposes a limitation not authorized by law be received if such restriction is to take effect or cease to be effective upon the happening of a contingency.[. . .]

6. When a point of order is made against any restriction on the expenditure of funds appropriated in a general appropriation bill on the ground that the restriction violates this rule, the rule shall be construed strictly and, in case of doubt, in favor of the point of order.

Table 2.2 The Rules of the House Governing Expired Authorizations

Rule XXI: RESTRICTIONS ON CERTAIN BILLS

2. (a) (1) An appropriation may not be reported in a general appropriation bill, and may not be in order as an amendment thereto, for an expenditure not previously authorized by law, except to continue appropriations for public works and objects that are already in progress.

(2) A reappropriation of unexpended balances of appropriations may not be reported in a general appropriation bill, and may not be in order as an amendment thereto, except to continue appropriations for public works and objects that are already in progress.

(b) A provision changing existing law may not be reported in a general appropriation bill, including a provision making the availability of funds contingent on the receipt or possession of information not required by existing law for the period of the appropriation, except germane provisions that retrench expenditures by the reduction of amounts of money covered by the bill . . . and except rescissions of appropriations contained in appropriation Acts.

(c) An amendment to a general appropriation bill shall not be in order if changing existing law. . . . Except as provided in paragraph (d), an amendment proposing a limitation not specifically contained or authorized in existing law for the period of the limitation shall not be in order during consideration of a general appropriation bill.

(d) After a general appropriation bill has been read for amendment, a motion that the Committee of the Whole House on the state of the Union rise and report the bill to the House with such amendments as may have been adopted shall, if offered by the Majority Leader or a designee, have precedence over motions to amend the bill. If such a motion to rise and report is rejected or not offered, amendments proposing limitations not specifically contained or authorized in existing law for the period of the limitation or proposing germane amendments that retrench expenditures by reductions of amounts of money covered by the bill may be considered.

As the floor manager for this bill, Congressman Joe Moakley (D-MA) explained after the rule was read on the floor:

> House Resolution 200 is the rule waiving points of order against certain pro-
> visions of the bill, H.R. 2942, the Department of Transportation and Related
> Agencies appropriations bill, for fiscal year 1992. . . . [It] waives clause 2 and
> 6 of rule XXI, against the entire bill. Clause 2 of rule XXI prohibits unautho-
> rized appropriations and legislative provisions in general appropriations bills.
> . . . The waivers are necessary because legislation for programs of the Coast
> Guard and surface transportation programs have not yet been enacted.[4]

The Rules Committee takes several factors into account when granting a waiver, including whether the authorizing committee has considered new authorization legislation that has been passed by the House but not enact-ed into law. Another factor the Rules Committee considers is how the waiver affects projects and programs in the districts of Rules Committee members. Special waivers are on occasion granted only to the programs or projects of committee members, and all other projects are left open to being stricken by a point of order (Tiefer 1989, 969–70). If an unauthorized program or project is not granted a waiver, members on the floor can strike the unauthorized appropriation from the bill. When an authorizing committee has not authorized a program, problems can ensue when an appropriations bill receives an open rule, as points of order can be brought against unauthorized spending. However, this spending potentially can be restored in a conference committee.[5]

How expired authorizations can cause problems in the appropriations process is illustrated in the following example. In 1993, the House Public Works Committee failed to authorize all components of the Department of Transportation. When the Appropriations Committee did not appro-priate funds for several grants important to Public Works Committee Chairman Norm Mineta (D-CA), he asked for and received an open rule for the appropriations bill. The open rule allowed Mineta to offer amend-ments to restore his projects, but it also allowed other members "to bring points of order against 18 unauthorized sections of the bill, including the entire office of the Transportation Secretary" (Congressional Quarterly Almanac [CQA] 1993, 668). Open warfare between the appropriators and authorization committee members ensued. This case shows that without a special or closed rule, authorizing committee members can be in a precar-ious position when they ask for an open rule if there are unauthorized appropriations contained in the bill.

The Senate has weaker rules regarding unauthorized appropriations (Tiefer 1989, 972–77). The initial clause of Senate Rule XVI is parallel to the

House rule forbidding unauthorized appropriations. Senators are able to raise points of order against such appropriations. However, subsequent clauses in the Senate rule create exceptions that make it easier for the Senate to consider unauthorized appropriations. Typically, the rule is waived as part of a unanimous consent agreement. As is the case in the House, the failure of authorizing committees to authorize legislation can be problematic when appropriations bills are being considered on the Senate floor.

Expired authorizations can also lead to the Appropriations Committee issuing bills that include legislative riders. Representative Harold Rogers (R-KY), chairman of the subcommittee that writes the Commerce-Justice-State appropriations, notes that when authorizing committees fail to reauthorize legislation, it puts pressure on the Appropriations Committee to legislate. Because there is no legislative vehicle other than the appropriations bill that will address the unauthorized legislation, members frequently offer substantive policy amendments—riders—to the appropriations bill for the unauthorized program (Meyers 1997). As Chairman Rogers explains, when an authorizing committee fails to take care of its business, that committee is saying to all members, "Come on, bring your riders. We've forgotten what [we] are supposed to do" (Baumann 1999, 691). Riders complicate the appropriations process and are an expression of a loss of control over the policy process by authorizing committees.

The Russell Amendment

In the postwar period, authorizing committees began to use short-term authorizations to change the policy landscape in Congress. As Fenno (1966) noted in his seminal work, *The Power of the Purse*, the use of short-term authorizations broke up the monopoly power that the Appropriations Committees had over information about various programs. Annual and multiyear authorizations served to "develop a body of subject-matter experts in addition to the Appropriations Committee" (Fenno 1966, 71). Authorizing committees were attempting to be seen within the chamber as the power brokers, the informational experts who could use their power to influence the appropriations process. This power move by authorizing committees, and the ability of these committees to complete their work in a timely manner, affected the business of appropriations in both the House and Senate.

These efforts were facilitated, in part, by the passage of the 1946 Legislative Reorganization Act. The act called on committees to "exercise continuous watchfulness of the execution . . . of any laws . . . by the agencies in the executive branch of the Government" (Aberbach 1990; see also

Galloway 1951).[6] Congress reiterated its desire to see committees perform effective oversight in 1971 when it amended the 1946 act (Aberbach 1979). These two laws were intended to build the capacities within Congress for committees to conduct oversight. Although some scholars of the oversight process have argued that Congress has not fulfilled its mandate to perform "continuous watchfulness" (e.g., Dodd and Schott 1979; Ogul 1976; Scher 1963), this view is undermined by data showing that the amount of oversight Congress conducts has increased dramatically over time. From the early 1960s to the mid-1980s, the number of days of oversight conducted by congressional committees increased by more than 300 percent. Oversight went from being less than one-tenth of the workload for congressional committees to being more than one-quarter of all activity (Aberbach 1990, 34–39). Also, it should not be forgotten that one of the most effective means of conducting oversight is to legislate. As McCubbins (1985) notes, legislation allows Congress to place controls on the implementation mechanisms available to agencies. Congress can delegate powers through legislation or rein in powers that agencies have acquired.

The first major postwar program subject to a short-term authorization was the Marshall Plan (Cox 1996). By making the authorization for the 1947 Foreign Aid Act short-term, Republican members of Congress hoped to exert more control over the way in which President Truman implemented it. The initial one-year authorization ensured that every year Congress would review how the Economic Recovery Agency was implementing the aid package to rebuild Europe and would be involved in any policy changes that were necessary as the conditions in Europe changed. The State Department would be limited in its ability to act unilaterally, and the foreign policy authorizing committees would exercise greater control over the monies that were expended and the form of these expenditures.

The Marshall Plan was a relatively unique use of short-term authorizations in the early postwar period. However, Senator Richard Russell (D-GA) set the stage for a broader change in the authorization environment when he added an amendment to the Military Construction Authorization Act for fiscal year 1960 that stated "[n]o funds may be appropriated after December 31, 1960 . . . for the procurement of aircraft, missiles, or naval vessels unless the appropriation of such funds has been authorized by legislation enacted after such date" (Dawson 1962, 42). This amendment was designed to make the Armed Services Committee a more powerful player in the debate over military policy. In his case study of this change in defense policy making, Dawson (1962, 42) argues that

> [the Russell amendment] served to break the monopoly long held by the annual Department of Defense Appropriations Act as the single regular

confrontation of Congress, as a decision-making participant through its Appropriations Committees, with the strategic issues and choices contained in defense policy.

Perhaps the most interesting aspect of Russell's efforts to move important components of the defense authorization to an annual appropriation is that Russell, and the other senators who developed the proposal, served on both the Armed Services Committee and the Appropriations Committee. Dawson argues that these senators made the defense authorization subject to an annual review because they wanted to exert more influence over defense policy and the military establishment. The existing system of having defense policy analyzed annually by the Appropriations Committee was not providing the oversight and policy control that these senators desired. Dawson (1962, 44) notes that

> [control over defense appropriations] has been a disappointing instrumentality.... [Senators] have, and can have, no adequate facilities for formulating alternative programs [to the administration's proposal] in any systematic fashion.

Defense appropriators recognized that they did not have the ability to evaluate defense policy in a comprehensive way, to determine the effectiveness of the various policies, and to craft alternative policies if necessary. The senators decided that in addition to the Appropriations Committee, the Armed Services Committee, which has jurisdiction over defense issues, should serve as a repository of expertise on defense policy. By having an annual authorization, Senator Russell envisioned that the Armed Services Committee would be able to analyze Department of Defense policy proposals and craft alternate proposals that could be considered by the appropriators. By dividing the labor between the authorization and Appropriations Committees, Congress would have two independent sources of expertise on defense policy, making it harder for the Department of Defense to exert undue control over defense policy vis-à-vis Congress.

One result of this change in authorization timing was to assist members in developing more expertise. "The authorization procedure lends itself to ['involving more Congressmen more immediately in the intellectual, technical, and political processes from which policy and strategy emerge'] because it possesses . . . the utility of focus" (Dawson 1962, 56). With all of the things going on in the Congress, a reauthorization focuses the mind because it puts a specific policy issue before members at a known time for them to deliberate.

The movement of defense policy from a permanent to a short-term authorization with the passage of Russell's amendment in 1959 began a larger trend toward the use of short-term authorizations by Congress. Russell's efforts to constrain defense policy through the use of short-term authorizations continued until, by the early 1980s, all defense programs were subject to annual authorization (Art 1985; Cox 1996). This trend also affected domestic discretionary programs, with most new agencies and programs created after 1960 having a short-term authorization. In addition, authorizing committees changed many existing agencies from permanent to short-term authorizations. Of the thirty-six new federal agencies created after 1960, only nine (25 percent) were given a permanent authorization (Cox 1996). Of the four cabinet level agencies that were created, only Housing and Urban Development and Education were given permanent authorizations. Between 1969 and 1978, the total number of programs with an annual authorization increased from approximately twelve to more than thirty, with many more programs having multiyear short-term authorizations. In fact, short-term authorizations had become so prevalent that by the 1970s, more than 25 percent of all laws enacted were reauthorizations (Schick 1983).

Variations in Authorizations

Today, the congressional landscape is filled with short-term authorizations, and there is great variation among them. Consider the following four federal programs and each program's form of authorization:

- The authorization for the Department of Defense lasts for only one year. The House and Senate Armed Services Committee must enact a new authorization for defense programs each year. These two committees are diligent in completing the defense authorization; the committee has never failed to renew the authorization.
- The authorization for surface transportation programs—which include highways, interstates, and public mass transit—historically has lasted for five or six years. The House Transportation and Infrastructure Committee and the Senate Environment and Public Works Committee have to act only twice in a decade to keep this program authorized. Similar to the defense committees, the committees with jurisdiction over surface transportation are diligent in enacting legislation renewing these programs, although the reauthorization legislation is often delayed for a short period as the authorizing committee fights to expand the size of the program.
- The Peace Corps began the 1990s with an expired authorization. In 1993 and 1995, the House International Relations Committee and the

Senate Foreign Relations Committee renewed the law reauthorizing the Peace Corps, but these renewals expired after only one year. Since 1996, the Peace Corps has operated with an expired authorization, which means that the legislative language authorizing appropriations for the program has expired, but these programs have received funding anyway because the rules governing unauthorized appropriations have been waived.

• Finally, the USA PATRIOT Act, passed in the aftermath of the September 11, 2001, terrorist attacks, contains numerous policy provisions that expire in 2005.

Any scholar interested in such issues as defense policy, foreign policy, transportation policy, education policy, welfare policy, environmental policy, regulatory policy, tax policy, and agriculture policy is studying programs and policies that function either totally or in part with short-term authorizations. The largest domestic discretionary programs are all subject to short-term authorizations. Defense policy is made in the annual defense authorization, as is foreign policy—as made in the Foreign Relations Authorization and Intelligence Authorization Acts. Air transportation and surface transportation—the largest domestic discretionary program— have short-term authorizations. Agriculture policy has one primary short-term authorization, but education policy has many, including the Elementary and Secondary Education Act, the Higher Education Act, the Vocational Education Act, and Individuals with Disability Education Act. Even tax policy is littered with taxes that have short-term authorizations, as readers of *Showdown at Gucci Gulch* (Birnbaum 1988) or followers of the 2001 Bush tax cut will remember. It is difficult to understand these policy areas without paying attention to and understanding how short-term authorizations impact policy making for the programs in these areas.

Short-term authorizations do not affect all policy areas. Many programs, especially entitlement programs that have permanent spending, are not subject to short-term authorizations. When considered in the context of the size of the federal government, this is not a trivial matter because entitlement programs account for more than half of all spending by the federal government. However, federal entitlement spending is limited to a small number of large programs such as Social Security. Entitlements remain outside the scope of the annual appropriations process, which is where the conflicts between authorizing and Appropriations Committees are played out. Thus, a study of short-term authorizations necessarily misses some components of the policy universe, but it still captures the majority of domestic and international programs the federal government administers. It also captures the only areas where legislators can control discretionary spending.

Summary

Tiefer (1989, 933) refers to short-term authorizations as an intrusion "on [the] appropriations' [committees] former monopoly on the annual review and expression of congressional views." Prior to the 1960s, the appropriations process was a primary locus of congressional review of programs and agencies. This is not to say that authorizing committees did not have hearings on these subjects, but they did not do so in a systematic or timely manner, except when a scandal occurred (Rockman 1984; Tiefer 1989). Thus, it was the appropriators, not the authorizers, who were best able to make adjustments to program policy and to expose program deficiencies.

Short-term authorizations helped authorizing committees shift the power back toward themselves. The authorizing committees were now able to gain the electoral benefits associated with legislative activity (e.g., Mayhew 1974). They also could attempt to put pressure on Appropriations Committees to fund programs at specific levels in order to achieve important program goals. After World War II, Congress first began to use short-term authorizations in foreign and defense policy, and then shifted their approach to the domestic policy arena. As the case of the Russell Amendment illustrates, this shift allowed authorizing committees to begin to exert more control over policies and programs under their jurisdiction. Policy committees were given greater incentives to acquire expertise and to use that expertise to influence the shape of existing programs under their jurisdiction on an ongoing basis.

3

Controlling Policy Change

For many programs, a short-term authorization is the mechanism for determining when explicit legislative action will take place and a bill will be enacted—that is, when policy change will occur. In this chapter I develop a conceptualization of short-term authorizations as a mechanism for controlling when legislative activity will occur in Congress. This conceptualization builds on existing literature regarding both agenda setting and congressional committee activity. Although policy scholars often discuss agenda setting and policy, few acknowledge the potential importance of short-term authorizations as a mechanism for controlling when change occurs. Similarly, congressional scholars often discuss the importance of rules, procedures, and institutions in the legislative process, but short-term authorizations have not been a part of this analysis, even though their use is both pervasive and rule-based. Short-term authorizations are a critical indicator for knowing when Congress will actually act on certain policy issues and when members will instead just discuss an issue but not act to change it.

A Conceptualization of Short-Term Authorizations as a Control Mechanism

Reelection is a primary goal of members of Congress, but achieving this goal requires the existence of certain conditions. For example, Mayhew (1974) and Fenno (1973) both identify several key behaviors that increase the likelihood of members achieving electoral success, in addition to achieving personal and professional success inside the institution. Although there are certain activities that members can do on their own—including giving speeches and introducing legislation—other activities need to be conducted within the context of the legislative process. Members, therefore, need to have regularized and predictable opportunities to engage in behaviors that benefit them both electorally and professionally, including the crafting of policy, taking positions on key issues, and claiming credit for bringing home projects and programs to their districts and states. A legislative mechanism that can allow members to engage the policy process in a meaningful way on a consistent basis is one that has great benefit to them.

Members also need to have a mechanism that allows them to make deals as a part of the legislative process and then to be certain that the gains made from policy trades and bargaining can be protected; that is, once they have engaged in the credit claiming and policy making, they need some assurance that their good works will not be undermined in ways that hinder their future electoral opportunities. As Weingast and Marshall (1988, 135) note, "[T]he institutions of the firm are designed, in part, to reduce the costs of assuring contractual performance." The question then becomes how to apply these lessons to legislatures. They note that some typical means of securing benefits in a legislature, such as vote trading, are not necessarily stable forms of interaction, arguing that (1988, 138–39),

> [Vote trading] assumes, for example, that all bills and their payoffs are noted in advance; that is, there are no random or unforeseen future events that may influence outcomes or payoffs. . . . A variety of exchange problems arise because the value of today's legislation significantly depends on next year's legislative events. . . . Because current legislators typically cannot bind a future legislative session, problems of enforcement over time are critically important for understanding legislatures and cannot be assumed away.

What legislators need, therefore, is a mechanism that binds a future legislative session, affords them regularized opportunities to engage in electorally beneficial activities, and ensures that they can minimize opportunities for other actors to renege on exchanges by changing the legislation containing the policy bargains. Weingast and Marshall implicitly suggest that this can be accomplished, in part, by planning in advance when future legislative action will occur. A mechanism that accomplishes this goal would have two qualities:

> 1. It would create highly dependable opportunities to engage in legislative activity.
> 2. It would ensure that any trades made at that time were secure for the duration of the trade; that is, everyone would receive the benefits that were promised before the legislation was again modified.

This description defines the essence of short-term authorizations. It is a mechanism whereby the legislative process for a specific program or policy is opened up for debate at a fixed point in time and, in the same legislation, a date is set for when future debate on the same policy or program will occur again. This is the type of planning that benefits legislators seeking reelection, who want a predictable political environment, and legislators who want to be able to ensure that the trades they make will remain in place.

Authorizing Policy: Short-Term Authorizations and Control

The use of short-term authorizations as a control mechanism by congressional committees raises a fundamental question: why do committees use short-term authorizations when doing so can in some way limit their future powers of gatekeeping? This is not a trivial question; many scholars have noted how the gatekeeping powers that committees have are a key source of power for committees. It is therefore important to understand why a rule or procedure that interferes or conflicts with the gatekeeping powers of committees is utilized by committees and included in many laws.

A committee's negative power to stop change in the policy areas under its jurisdiction is among its most important.[1] Gatekeeping affects several aspects of committee behavior, extending beyond the commonly understood power to decide whether or not to originate a piece of legislation (Deering and Smith 1997, 6–10). For example, a committee is typically sensitive to the type of rule a piece of legislation will receive (Denzau and Mackay 1983). Committees want legislation they originate to receive as restrictive a rule as possible in order to keep their mischievous colleagues from modifying it on the floor through amendments. They also want to be able to control the treatment of their legislation in conference committees (Shepsle and Wiengast 1987a, 1987b; cf. Krehbiel 1987).

A short-term authorization runs counter to gatekeeping because it mandates a certain date when an authorizing committee will consider legislation. As Kingdon (1995) notes, the renewal of a short-term authorization causes a predictable opening of the policy window. The committee, therefore, has to determine if it can address the policy issue without losing control of the legislation on the floor or creating a situation where policy stakeholders can use the reauthorization legislation as a vehicle for their own pet projects, which may run counter to the committee's policy preferences. The fact that authorizing committees use short-term authorizations even though it can disrupt these gatekeeping powers suggests that committees see a benefit to be gained by using this procedure, but the failure of many committees to reauthorize programs in a timely manner likewise suggests that problems can exist in opening up the policy process at fixed points in time, as reauthorization requires. Expired program authorizations reflect a conflict in an authorizing committee between a desire to exert ongoing control over an agency and a desire to use gatekeeping power to control policies emerging from its jurisdiction.

Forms of Control

The benefit of short-term authorizations for congressional committees is that it provides them with two important forms of control. First, it provides agenda control by channeling pressures for legislative activity into systematic, planned time frames—specifically, when the program authorization in question is set to expire. In this sense, short-term authorizations provide committees with a form of enhanced gatekeeping by constraining interest groups from pressing for policy change whenever it suits their interests. Committees can point to the authorization as the time—and the only time—when they will consider changes to an existing policy. Second, it provides for ongoing policy control. Members can use reauthorizations as a time for revising legislation in order to improve the program's implementation, to distribute benefits, and to either constrain or liberate the various actors involved in implementing the program. The alternative to short-term authorizations—random change whenever pressures become too great for member to ignore—would make for a system whereby programs might change randomly, but frequently, and no one in the process could be certain how long any given implementation structure, political deal, or programmatic change would remain in place.

Members of Congress have a variety of reasons for wanting systematic opportunities to revise legislation in a given policy area. Examining surface transportation policy (i.e., highway and transit policy), which is handled by the Transportation and Infrastructure (T&I) Committee (previously the Public Works Committee), provides an example of the benefits that arise from both planning opportunities to revise legislation and taking legislation off of policy agenda.

Consider first the advantages members gain from revising legislation at planned intervals. For members of the T&I Committee, the six-year surface transportation authorization well serves the needs of members with high demands for transportation.[2] During the reauthorization process, the legislation being crafted has specific provisions of importance to members, as there are peculiar benefits that individual members can ascertain through the distribution of "high priority projects." Projects have value to the members, helping them to achieve their reelection goals, allowing them to engage in credit claiming, position taking, advertising, and the making of good public policy, at least in their districts (Fenno 1973; Mayhew 1974). By distributing these projects with some regularity (roughly twice a decade), the T&I Committee can give all members several "bites at this apple" during their service in Congress. When transportation projects are not being allocated, another committee, perhaps agriculture or education, is distributing some benefit through a different reauthorization, from which members can profit.

Projects are not only valuable to members who receive them, but they also have value to a committee which distributes them because they are an important tool in building winning policy coalitions (e.g., Evans 1994) and helping committee members increase their own influence as they vote on which members get projects. The power of the Transportation and Infrastructure/Public Works Committees is largely based on the power of the committee members, especially senior members, to determine the distribution of projects. It is generally recognized that Jim Wright became majority leader in the late 1970s because of the tremendous power base he developed as a senior member of the Public Works Committee. The vote on leaders that year occurred roughly concomitantly with the reauthorization of various surface transportation programs (CQA 1977).

Second, once deals have been struck and transportation projects have been distributed—and broader determinations have been made about how the transportation funding formulas will distribute billions of dollars each year among states and localities—the members have an incentive for surface transportation policy to be taken off the legislative agenda so that their deals do not unravel. With a short-term authorization, committee members can point to an authorization's expiration as the time where those who want to change the policy can know that they will have an opportunity to change it, thus relieving the obligation to change the policy whenever pressure groups demand.

Examining the workload of committees in a given policy area is one way of seeing how short-term authorizations serve to place items on the legislative agenda and then take them off the agenda. Figure 3.1 shows the schedule of program authorizations for education policy for the years 1992 through 2002. Consider, for example, three key education programs: Head Start, the Individuals with Disabilities Education Act (IDEA), and the Elementary and Secondary Education Act (ESEA). Note how Head Start is on the legislative agenda in 1994 and then not on the agenda again until 1998. Similarly, ESEA is on the agenda in 1993, extended for one year to 1994, and then taken off the agenda until 2000. Finally, IDEA is on the agenda in 1994 but then is off the agenda until its authorization expires in 2002.

Figure 3.1 Education Programs and the Year Their Authorization Expired

Year	Programs
1992	Dropout Prevention Reauthorization of the Tribally Controlled College Act Higher Education Act
1993	STAR Schools Drug Free Schools Elementary and Secondary Education Act (ESEA)
1994	National Center for Education Statistics Individuals with Disabilities Education Act (IDEA) Even Start Head Start Library Services and Construction Act Drug Free Schools Elementary and Secondary Education Act (ESEA) School to Work Grants
1995	Library Services and Construction Act National Literacy Act School to Work Grants Vocational and Applied Technology Education
1996	National and Community Service Trust Act Adult Education Act Environmental Education Act
1997	National Assessment of Educational Progress Higher Education Amendments
1998	National Education Goals Panel Head Start
1999	Even Start National Center for Education Statistics Bilingual Education Impact Aid School to Work Grants
2001	Charter School Education Program
2002	Individuals with Disabilities Education Act (IDEA) Library Services and Construction Act

Similar findings arise when considering the legislation that is reported from committee. Figure 3.2 shows all bills that were reported out of the House Education and the Workforce Committee from the 103rd to 107th Congresses. Program reauthorizations tend to make up a large number of the bills considered each Congress, with the exception of the 104th Congress. By examining the content of these bills more closely, it is also possible to discern that these reauthorization bills also tend to be the larger policy issues considered by the committee.

Figure 3.2 All Education Bills, House Education Committee 103rd through
         107th Congresses

Congress	Education Bills
103rd Congress	HR 6—extends Elementary and Secondary Education Act (ESEA) R HR 8—amends Children Nutrition Act of 1966 and National School Lunch Act **R** HR 1804—provides framework for all federal education programs HR 2339— Technology Assistance for Individuals with Disabilities R HR 2351—arts foundations, humanities, and museum services R HR 2884—develops School to Work Opportunities in all states HR 4250—appropriates for Head Start and community service R
104th Congress	HR 1557—National Foundation on Arts and Humanities Act R HR 1617—consolidates vocational and adult education R HR 1720—cuts federal funding for part of Higher Education Act HR 2066—gives schools more flexibility in providing meals HR 3055—continues grant to historically black graduate schools HR 3268—amends and funds IDEA R HR 3269—amends Impact Aid Program HR 3863—allows lenders to pay origination fees on unsubsidized loans
105th Congress	HR 5 —amends and funds IDEA R HR 6—Higher Education Act R HR 914—corrects graduation data disclosures HR 1385—consolidates adult education programs R HR 1853—amends vocational and applied technology act R HR 2535—consolidates student loans into two programs R HR 2614—improves literacy through teacher training HR 2616—improves and expands charter schools HR 2846—no funding for national testing HR 3248—education funding HR 3254—clarifies state IDEA requirements HR 3892—establishes program for children learning English
106th Congress	HR 2—education funding R HR 800—provides education flexibility partnerships HR 1995—empowers and trains teachers R HR 2300—allows states to combine some education funds HR 3222—family literacy projects R HR 3616—continues impact aid R HR 4141—amends Elementary and Secondary Act (ESEA) R HR 4504—technical adjustments, Higher Education Act
107th Congress	HR 1—accountability and choice, no child left behind (ESEA) R HR 1992—more telecom higher education HR 3394—computer and network security R&D HR 3784—extends Museum and Library Services Act R HR 3801—improves federal education research and statistics

Note: **R** means that the legislation is part of a reauthorization.

Agenda Dynamics

Various scholars have attempted to explain the policy-making process;
most have focused on specific aspects of the process. Systems theorists,
such as Easton (1957) and Lasswell and Kaplan (1950), and historical insti-
tutionalists, such Skowronek and Orren (1994) or Steinmo et al. (1992),
attempt to explain the interaction between institutional structures and

political decision making. Other analysts, such as Kingdon (1995) and Rochefort and Cobb (1994), identify and explain specific elements of the process (i.e., problem definition, policy formulation, and agenda setting).

A common approach is to focus on the agenda-setting aspects of the policy process. This literature is often focused on agenda setting within specific institutions. For example, studies of executive branch agencies often focus on their ability to serve as agenda setters because of their informational expertise (e.g., Niskanen 1971; cf. Eavey and Miller 1984). Likewise, studies of presidential attention to issues consider the important role that the president plays in setting the tone for the agenda in Washington (e.g., Cohen 1995; Light 1991; Wood and Peake 1998). Works studying Congress (e.g., Bendor and Moe 1986; Fox and Clapp 1970; King 1996) often focus on the agenda control capacities of congressional committees. This power manifests through committee jurisdictional boundaries and their institutional powers (e.g., the Rules Committee). Members also tailor this agenda as they attempt to achieve their personal and political goals (e.g., Fenno 1973; Mayhew 1974; Mouw and MacKuen 1992). Agenda setting on the courts has often examined the role that interest groups play in affecting agenda setting on the Supreme Court (e.g., Calderia and Wright 1988, 1990; McGuire and Calderia 1993) or the ability of court members to engage in issue expansion and directed policy change (McGuire and Palmer 1996).

Examinations of agenda setting across institutions have typically left out the courts and focused directly on presidential-congressional relations. Here, it is the president, not the Congress, who is seen as being the key agenda setter. Part of this focus comes from the fact that agenda setting is one of the key powers of the president (e.g., Bond and Fleisher 1990; Edwards 1989). Thus, studies of agenda setting across institutions center on the ability of the president to focus the attention of Congress on specific issues (e.g., Edwards and Wood, 1999). When all three institutions have been examined together (e.g., Fleming, Wood, and Bohnte 1999), the examination has been of issue attention, examining important policy areas—civil rights, civil liberties, and the environment—but this macro focus limits the ability to examine how attention transforms itself into programmatic action by institutions.

Few scholars of the agenda-setting process consider short-term authorizations in their analysis. One who does is Kingdon (1995), who provides a theory of agenda setting in the federal policy process in his book *Agendas, Alternatives, and Public Policy.* He argues that the federal agenda-setting process is a "primordial soup," with three factors, or "streams of processes," influencing it: problems, policies, and politics. Participants in the policy process—including lobbyists, members of Congress, agency personnel, White House personnel, think tank members, and academics—attempt to manipulate these streams to affect the policy agenda in Washington. What these policy players need in order to get their ideas moving is an opening in a "policy window." This window is "an opportunity for advocates of proposals to push their pet solutions, or to push attention to their special problems" (Kingdon 1995, 165).

According to Kingdon, there are two types of policy windows. The first kind is the unpredictable window that opens in response to other events, such as a change in administration, change in partisan control of Congress, change in the national mood on a specific issue, or a national crisis. When these windows open—and Kingdon argues that they do not stay open for long—political stakeholders have to be prepared to push their agenda item through that opening. Kingdon suggests that these unpredictable windows mostly open by accident, and that when they do, policy stakeholders have to act quickly because one can never know if the opportunity for action will occur again in the near future. Downs (1972) makes a similar argument about the agenda process, presenting a five-stage theory that focuses on the interrelationship between the media and the public's perception of public policies.

The second type of policy window is the predictable window, which opens when a scheduled event occurs. Scheduled events would include the president's State of the Union Address and changes in congressional sessions or presidential terms. Kingdon (1995, 186–88) also notes that the reauthorization of a program constitutes a predictable window opening. For stakeholders inside and outside of Congress, reauthorizations are likely to be the most common and reliable chance to promote activity in a given policy area, as a reauthorization is likely to produce a legislative vehicle for related issues. Kingdon (1995) provides two examples from his research of short-term authorizations as predictable windows: health manpower issues and surface transportation. Medical manpower issues were quite prominent in 1976, and surface transportation issues were quite prominent in 1978. His analysis, based on interviews with policy makers, is that activity occurred in both cases because these issues were up for reauthorization in those years. In each case, the expiration of the short-term authorization set off a flurry of activity among legislators, interest groups, and agency personnel. The expiration of these short-term authorizations almost certainly guaranteed that the authorizing committee would consider legislation to reauthorize the program, and this would create a legislative vehicle upon which interested parties could attempt to attach their own pet project. One interesting aspect of Kingdon's finding regarding increased levels of health manpower activity in 1976 and transportation policy activity in 1978 is that he could have known this was likely to occur when he was planning his study because the decision to reauthorize these two programs had been made earlier.

Although his book focuses more on unpredictable windows as opposed to predictable ones, Kingdon does not provide any analysis of which is more likely to produce actual policy change through legislative activity. Implicit in Kingdon's (1995) argument is the idea that the appropriations process creates an opening in policy windows in all policy areas. Because annual appropriations affect most areas of domestic and foreign affairs, these bills create an opportunity for making policy change. However, he does not pursue the differences between authorization and appropriations windows in his discussion. Regardless of where the predictable opening occurs, groups are interested in utilizing windows that are as predictable as possible, as opposed to hoping that an unplanned event will occur to create an opening.

Policy windows that open must eventually close. In his survey of policy stakeholders, Kingdon observed that interest in an issue falls after the reauthorization process ends. "Without the prospect of an open window, participants [in the given policy area] slack off" (Kingdon 1995, 167). When Congress reauthorizes a policy for a given period, the committees of jurisdiction will not consider issues related to the reauthorized policy again until it is time for the current authorization to expire. After the reauthorization, little legislative activity in that policy area will occur until the program is authorized again.

Longitudinal Change

While Kingdon studied short-term agenda dynamics, more recent studies of the policy process have moved from short cross-sectional analyses to longitudinal analyses of agenda change. Among the first scholars to do this were Baumgartner and Jones (1993) in their analysis of the factors that lead to instability in agendas over time. They argue that the focus on incrementalism and stability in the policy process has led scholars to overlook the "punctuations"—large shifts in policy dynamics—in the policy equilibria over time. Baumgartner and Jones see policy stability arising, in part, because a limited number of stakeholders come to dominate a given policy area, gaining "monopoly control" over the issue area. The stakeholders in the policy monopoly are able to define the policy in a specific way, and that policy definition remains the dominant view of the issue by most stakeholders in the issue area (e.g., Edelman 1985; Stone 1997). These stakeholders are also able to control the venue—for example, the congressional committee—in which the policy is discussed. Iron triangles or issue networks can be understood as often being a part of, or supporting, a policy monopoly (Browne and Paik 1993). As long as the policy monopoly exists, change in the given issue area is likely to occur incrementally, if any change occurs at all.

However, the policy world is dynamic, and a policy monopoly can deteriorate over time. Several factors can facilitate dramatic change in a policy area. New stakeholders can be mobilized and enter the policy debate. These new stakeholders then are likely to attempt to change the policy definition of the issue, from one favorable to the existing coalition to one more favorable to the newly mobilized stakeholders. The newly mobilized are also likely to seek out new venues for this debate. As a policy comes to prominence in the public agenda, or as it comes to be viewed by the public and policy stakeholders in a different light, "existing policies can be either reinforced or questioned. Reinforcement creates great obstacles to anything but modest change, but the questioning of policies at the most fundamental levels creates opportunities for reversals in policy outcomes" (True, Jones, and Baumgartner 1999, 97–98). At some point, the pressure in the policy area can become too great, and the policy may change dramatically (a punctuation in the previous state of equilibrium) and then stabilize again.

Baumgartner and Jones support their theory with an analysis of change in several policy areas—including nuclear energy, pesticides, and tobacco—over the postwar years. (It is interesting here to note that throughout the 1960s and 1970s, the Nuclear Regulatory Commission was governed by a short-term authorization, a factor not considered by Baumgartner and Jones in their analysis.) For example, as they track pesticide policy over time, they find that there is a rapid growth in the volume of hearings on this topic beginning in the late 1960s and that the tone of these hearings was highly skewed toward disapproval of pesticides and pesticide use. Concomitant with this trend was a similar shift in media coverage of pesticides. Through the early 1960s, media coverage of pesticides tended to be mostly positive. However, by the late 1960s, the coverage was much more evenly divided, with more articles taking a negative tone toward pesticides. Baumgartner and Jones note that this shift in the environment both resulted from and created opportunities for more effective mobilization by opponents to widespread pesticide use. This period is one when legislative activity occurs to regulate pesticide, although their analysis does not statistically link policy change and legislative activity or consider whether reauthorizations lead to a pattern of recurring policy change.

A second, related model of policy change over time is a component of a larger theory of the policy process that has been developed by Sabatier and Jenkins-Smith (1993). Their advocacy coalition framework (ACF) is intended to be a broad theory of the policy process that goes beyond the often-used description of the policy process as a series of stages, including agenda setting, implementation, and evaluation. What they desired instead was to create a dynamic theory of the policy process that is nuanced and can better explain the factors that influence changes in public policy over time. Different scholars have tested various aspects of the ACF theory in more than thirty different academic studies (Sabatier and Jenkins-Smith 1999).

The ACF views the policy process quite broadly, both in terms of how policy networks are defined and the size of the policy domains studied. This theory typically examines policy change by studying policy domains (e.g., education policy) and not a program or institution, such as education for the disabled or education policy within the U.S. Department of Education. It is not that the disabled or the department are not important components to education policy, but a broader examination of education policy is needed to appreciate why specific changes occur in these programs. Similarly, the policy networks they examine are quite broad as well. Important stakeholders in the policy process include not only the usual suspects—interest groups, legislators, and administrative agencies—but also journalists, policy analysts, researchers, and stakeholders from all levels of government. These different groups all contribute to the understanding of an issue and often try to shape public perceptions through their pronouncements and actions.

As these groups work to shape policy, they also add to the general knowledge about an issue. The ACF is premised on the idea that policy change is based on learning that comes from the availability of technical information about the policy issue in question. Scientific analyses and other studies often change the collective perceptions of an issue as new information comes to the fore. This information also shapes the understanding of how an issue is interrelated and the ways in which the problem can best be addressed. Specifically, Sabatier and Jenkins-Smith (1999, 119–20) believe that public policies "incorporate specific theories about how to achieve their objectives [and] involve value priorities, perceptions of important causal relationships . . . and perceptions . . . concerning the efficacy of various policy instruments." Not surprisingly, changes in technical knowledge can change perceptions of an issue and the understanding of the causal relationships that underlie a policy problem.

As with the punctuated equilibrium theory, the ACF theory is predicated on a belief that the key to understanding policy change is to examine a given policy area for an extended period. Time is required to see how the stakeholders involved in the policy process in a given domain aggregate into advocacy coalitions. These coalitions consist of like-minded stakeholders who work together to make policy change and are held together because the coalition members all believe in a similar theory about how the policy should be designed and implemented. Coalition members contribute to the understanding of the issue through their research and their public efforts to frame the issue in terms most favorable to them.

The success or failure of these coalitions is based, in part, on their ability to shape the debate in terms that favor their theory of policy. One thing that groups do in their efforts to achieve success is to "venue shop" in order to find a political institution that supports their worldview. For example, transportation groups want their issue addressed by an agency or level of government that most supports their view of what transportation policy should be. In general, there is a perception that state transportation departments view transportation as being a highway capacity problem, based on their historical role in building roads that dates back to their initial inception as state highway departments. Conversely, cities are often viewed as being hostile to road building and being much more interested in building transit systems. Not surprisingly, road advocates tend to like to see transportation policy made at the state level, but environmental and transit groups tend to like to see cities more involved in the process. Decisions about which venue is appropriate are often established in law, as one coalition or another attempts to lock in an advantage they have regarding where policy decisions are made.

Defining Policy Change

The policy literature defines policy change in a variety of ways. In the punctuated equilibrium theory, policy change occurs when there is a change in the way a policy is framed, as noted by rapid changes in media coverage or in the hearing environment in Congress. For example, media coverage of the issue may shift from being positive or neutral to being sharply negative, and the volume of media coverage may rise. The advocacy coalition framework uses a similar definition of policy change, which is related to changes in the composition of the advocacy coalitions or in scientific and public knowledge. Other scholars (e.g., Weingast 1984) note that oversight hearings, in and of themselves, often shape the behavior of agencies, because they signal to agencies the desires of committee members and contain an implicit threat of retaliation if these views are not appropriately taken into account. Likewise, scholars of bureaucratic politics point to rule making (e.g., Kerwin 1999) and administrative discretion (e.g., Bawn 1995; Epstein and O'Halloran 1994; Wilson 1989) as points where policy change occurs.

There are other means of defining policy change. The common alternate definition—which is the definition used in this analysis—that has been used by political scientists studying policy change in Congress (e.g., Brady and Sinclair 1984; Krehbiel 1998) is to define policy change as occurring when new legislation affecting a given policy area is enacted. One benefit of this definition is that it is clearly measurable; the statutory authority underlying an agency or program is actually changed. This definition is also important to policy stakeholders and members of Congress. Changes in the law allow one set of stakeholders to establish their gains in law. Any subsequent change in policy requires the losing set of stakeholders to develop their own winning coalition that is able to move the status quo. Legislative changes also allow members to engage in distributive politics, in the position taking, advertising, and credit claiming that are important for electoral success and in the internal politics that allow members to gain power within the chamber (Fenno 1973; Mayhew 1974). From a policy standpoint, the substance of legislative changes is important for members as well. Legislative action allows various ex ante and ongoing controls to be placed on an agency or policy (Balla 1998; Epstein and O'Halloran 1994; McCubbins 1985; McCubbins, Noll, and Weingast 1987). There are critics of this definition, such as Sabatier and Jenkins-Smith (1999), who argue that most legal changes are incremental. However, incremental changes can have dramatic effects for policy stakeholders. For example, incremental changes in a funding formula can result in revenue shifts totaling tens of millions of dollars or can completely shut certain policy actors out of the implementation process.

The validity of this definition of policy change was confirmed in numerous interviews held with interest group members, agency personnel, and congressional staff. These individuals involved in the federal policy process noted that reauthorization legislation is the most common and most powerful vehicle for facilitating policy change. One agency staffer noted that "everything needs a vehicle, and the reauthorization bills are the biggest around."[3] Reauthorization bills are especially important for members of the minority party in the House. As one minority party staffer who handles education policy noted, "[F]or people in the minority, life is driven by reauthorizations because they are the main vehicles that will come out of committee."[4]

As it so happens, for almost all major public policies—from agriculture to defense to transportation—the process of a short-term authorization expiring is the most common opportunity for a policy window to open, creating the possibility for actual policy change through legislative activity to occur. Obviously, there are other means of changing policy that do not include legislative activity, such as executive orders, administrative rule making, and the like. However, most dramatic policy change, and even activities as simple as reorganizing an agency or a program, require congressional approval. This makes a short-term authorization similar to a lock on a vault that is set to open at a specified time. Only when the timer goes off and the vault doors open can anyone hope to get to the treasure— in this case, to have their desired policy outcome enacted in law. Whichever side won the policy debate the last time serves as a guard, trying to keep change from occurring as their opponents fight to steal away with the outcome they want.

Neither the ACF nor punctuated equilibrium theories consider whether reauthorizations are a point that policy stakeholders recognize as being strategic for making dramatic policy change. This failure to consider the role of short-term authorizations in the process of policy change is more exceptional considering that both theories have been directly tested on programs with short-term authorizations. However, neither the short-term authorization mechanism nor the authorization status of the programs in question were variables considered in the analysis.

Over the long term, reauthorizations are one of the most consistent and important opportunities to change public policy available to groups in most policy areas. Consider, for instance, the 1991 reauthorization of the federal surface transportation programs (i.e., highways and transit) and how it fits into both the ACF and punctuated equilibrium theories. The environmental groups that had just finished work lobbying on the Clean Air Act Amendments used this "open window" to make the transportation reauthorization into a vehicle for environmental activism. Working through Senator Daniel Patrick Moynihan (D-NY), the environmentalists used the Senate Environment and Public Works Committee, which has a broader jurisdiction than its House counterpart (previously named the House Public Works Committee), as a venue for changing the issue in the 1991 reauthorization from building roads to mitigating the environmental impact of highways (CQA 1991).

In this example, the expiration of the surface transportation authorization created the opportunity for one advocacy coalition to change the monopoly view of transportation as being an issue of moving people and goods around the country to one of moving people and goods in an environmentally sound manner. More importantly, the winners in the debate were able to lock in their gains through legislative action, ensuring that all states and localities would have to act as the winning coalition desired. This legislative win made it almost impossible for advocates on the other side to venue shop, to reframe the debate, and to change the view of the issue until the next authorization, or even longer. Without this (fortuitously timed) opportunity that arose from an action scheduled in law by a congressional committee five years earlier, the environmental groups might not have had the chance to promote these changes. In addition, it is not clear that changes in policy equilibria occur outside of the reauthorization process. Information is lacking about whether the learning that goes on about a policy, or changes in a policy's definition by the public, lead to changes in the law when there is an existing short-term authorization that is scheduled to expire at some point in the relatively near future.

Summary

Short-term authorizations are important not just as an agenda-setting tool but as an agenda-control tool. They provide congressional committees with a form of enhanced gatekeeping powers, channeling policy change into a specific time point. The expiration of a short-term authorization is perhaps the single most common predictable opening of a policy window for most federal programs. These openings are critical points in the policy process for the various stakeholders in advocacy coalitions, who are attempting to lock in their view of the policy world through legislative activity. Short-term authorizations do not just result in issues being put on the table; they also are a mechanism for forcing policy action. Once this action occurs, the length of the authorization shuts the door on legislative activity in that area during the interim. By taking the issue off the agenda for this specified time period, members—and outside stakeholders on each side of an issue—can be confident that the agreements that have been made will remain in place until the scheduled end of the authorization.

The idea of policy control from short-term authorizations fits into existing theories of policy change, but has never been studied in that context. Short-term authorizations are congruous with there being "punctuated equilibria" in the policy process, as well as in policy change and learning. In fact, the reauthorization process can enhance our understanding of how the overall policy change process functions. Between authorizations, groups and members can work to shape the policy environment. For example, this is when environmental groups would press for hearings opposing pesticides and work the media to change the public's perception on the topic. Then, at the reauthorization, groups and members can press for changes that build upon the policy framing that they have developed.

Signaling to Appropriators: Who's Listening?

"I think most people realize [that an authorization] is only a hunting
license for an appropriation."
—Senator Mark O. Hatfield (R-OR), former Chairman of the Senate
Appropriations Committee.

Senator Hatfield's sentiments reflect the dynamics of the appropriations
process, as understood by an appropriator. The books that comprise the
U.S. Code are filled with programs that Congress has created. The question
is, what programs will get how much money? Today, the division of labor,
as set forth in the committee structure, is that appropriators make those
decisions for all discretionary spending. It is the Appropriations
Committees that write the appropriations bills and determine how funding is allocated. The benefits of being an appropriator are obvious; as one
transportation lobbyist, who is also a former congressional staffer said,
"Part of [making funding decisions] is ego for being an appropriator. They
just want to be able to control the money."[1] Although some scholars have
argued that appropriators, especially in the House, well serve the majority
party, authorizing committee members are often less than pleased with the
level of funding that their programs receive (Keiweit and McCubbins
1991). This is not just true now; ever since there have been appropriators
there have been battles over how appropriation funds are allocated.

One way that authorizing committee members can attempt to influence
appropriations levels is to signal to appropriators what level of funding they
think a given program should receive. Short-term authorizations have been
seen as one such signaling mechanism. In this chapter, I examine the relative
efficacy of this signaling model in order to discern whether the signaling
efforts of authorizing committees are heard in the hearing rooms and staff

offices of the Appropriations Committees. I also consider whether the authorization status of a program affects the appropriation it receives. However, before I delve into these results, it is first beneficial to understand some of the history of the animosity that exists between authorizers and appropriators.

Appropriations Battles in Context

The Constitution does not require that legislation authorizing spending and legislation appropriating funds be considered separately. However, these two activities generally have been kept distinct. For example, the first Congress authorized the creation of a War Department and then appropriated funds separately for its operation (Schick 1995, 110). Thus, passing authorization legislation is the first step in the budget process; once it has a legal basis from which to operate, it is generally eligible to receive an appropriation (Fisher 1979; Meyers 1988; Oleszek 1989; Schick 1980, 1995; Tiefer 1989). One reason for separating authorizations and appropriations is to keep Congress from agreeing to an inferior policy choice in order to ensure the funding of government operations (Schick 1995); policy and fiscal conflicts can be conducted in separate venues. However, this separation is much clearer in theory than in practice (Fisher 1979), and it is often inefficient, leading some scholars (e.g., Meyers 1997) to suggest combining appropriations and authorization functions.

Although the House and Senate separated program authorization decisions from appropriations decisions starting with the First Congress, congressional rules have not always reflected this division between appropriations and authorizations. It took more than one hundred years before both the House and the Senate developed committees with complete and unique jurisdiction over appropriations decisions (e.g., Fisher 1979; Ippolito 1981; Stewart 1989; Tiefer 1989). The House Ways and Means Committee, which initially had jurisdiction over revenue and appropriations decisions, was made a standing committee in 1802. In the Senate, prior to the establishment of the Finance Committee in 1816, select committees handled appropriations bills. However, only in the 1830s did the Senate consolidate all appropriations in the Finance Committee, with appropriations for the Navy, Revolutionary War Pensions, and implementation of American Indian treaties being the last to be subsumed into the Finance Committee's jurisdiction.

The creation of appropriations committees led to intense competitions for power between appropriators and authorizers, and with these rivalries came rules to govern legislative action (Burkhead 1956; Fisher 1979; Ippolito 1981; Oleszek 1989, 51; Stewart 1989; Tiefer 1989). In 1837, the

House adopted a rule stating, "No appropriation shall be reported in such general appropriation bills, or be in order as an amendment thereto, for any expenditure not previously authorized by law" (Fisher 1979, 54–55). One year later, the House modified the rule to allow unauthorized appropriations "in continuation of appropriations for such public works and objects as are already in progress and for contingencies for carrying on the several departments of government" (Fisher 1979, 55). These rules were adopted because House members were adding riders for unauthorized appropriations to appropriations bills, and the Senate was rejecting them, and this interchamber conflict over House riders was delaying the appropriations process.

The Senate adopted similar rules against unauthorized appropriations ten years later, when they began to interfere with the Senate's efficient operation. In the aftermath of the Mexican War, senators began to bring forth private claims on the government on behalf of constituents. When the claims could not pass on their own merits, senators would add them to appropriations bills as amendments. In the high-deficit times that followed the war, these private claims stressed the budget, and in 1850 the Senate adopted a new rule disallowing all unauthorized appropriations except those funding existing laws. Standing committees in the Senate were allowed to recommend unauthorized appropriations when the rule was modified in 1852.

The new rules barring unauthorized appropriations enhanced the power of authorizing committees, who were able to raise a point of order whenever members outside the committee attempted to tread on their jurisdictional turf. It enhanced their gatekeeping powers as well by keeping members outside the committee, or even individual members on the committee, from dictating spending for programs that had not been approved by a majority of all committee members. Prohibiting unauthorized appropriations provided a simple yet effective means of ensuring that committees could set policy within their jurisdictions without being undercut through backdoor legislative efforts, such as unauthorized appropriations.

To address the large debt that resulted from the Civil War, the House and Senate created Appropriations Committees. Congressional leaders thought that the new committees would create efficiencies by dividing appropriations and taxation policy; Appropriations Committees would focus solely on constraining spending. Not surprisingly, this focus on controlling spending created tensions between the authorizing and Appropriations Committees (Ippolito 1981; Stewart 1989). Perhaps the most controversial power was given to the House Appropriations Committee, where the Holman Amendment gave the committee the power to change existing authorization laws if it would result in cost savings being achieved. When the Appropriations Committee used this power to interfere with the operations of authorizing committees, there was a general rebellion against the appropriators. Starting in the late 1870s, authorizing committees had programs and policies they deemed important removed from the jurisdiction of the Appropriations Committees, and spending for those programs increased dramatically. For example, spending for rivers and harbors roughly doubled—increasing from $7.4 million to $13.6 million annually—almost immediately after the Appropriations Committees lost control of this policy (Ippolito 1981).

Congress has continued to wrestle with how to balance authorization and appropriations issues. In 1921 Congress passed the Budget and Accounting Act (BAA), to systematically structure the executive-congressional relationship for the appropriations and budget processes (Shuman 1992, 25–33). The BAA created the Bureau of the Budget and the General Accounting Office and provided a structure to the executive side of the budget process. In 1974, Congress passed the Congressional Budget and Impoundment Control Act (CBICA) to create a meaningful budget process internal to Congress (Collender 1997; Havemann 1978; Oleszek 1989). In addition to creating new institutions within the legislative branch—including the Congressional Budget Office and the House and Senate Budget Committees—the CBICA was designed to provide structure and a timetable to the budgeting, authorization, and appropriations processes. Authorizations were to be completed in a timely manner, prior to the completion of the appropriations process, so appropriations could be made based on complete information. However, authorization legislation is often completed concomitantly with appropriations bills (CBO 2003; Fisher 1983; Meyers 1997, 1988). This is especially true for programs with an annual authorization, such as the defense authorization.

Although the CBICA did not change the balance of power between appropriators and authorizers, the 1990 Budget Enforcement Act (BEA) did change the dynamic between these rivals (Collender 1997, esp. chap. 5; Thurber 1997). After the failure of the Gramm-Rudman-Hollings Act (GRH) to reduce the deficit by setting specific deficit targets for each fiscal year, the BEA focused on reducing the deficit by limiting discretionary spending each year. The responsibility for controlling the deficits rested in the Appropriations Committees; the BEA placed caps on appropriations for various categories of discretionary spending and gave appropriators the responsibility for determining how to keep spending under each discretionary spending cap. The Appropriations Committees were responsible for balancing the levels of funding received by all programs, regardless of the amounts authorized. Appropriators did not always stay within the funding caps, but the law formally shifted power to the Appropriations Committees.

The Authorization as Signaling Model

The separation of the authorization and appropriations processes creates conflict between authorization and appropriation committees. Although the Budget Committee theoretically is responsible for developing an overall spending plan for Congress, it is the appropriators who have to make the budget framework meaningful. Additionally, appropriators do not always feel constrained by any budget agreement. Authorizers want the programs under their jurisdiction funded at certain specified levels; appropriators have to balance spending requests from various actors in order to develop a comprehensive spending plan for the federal government. More specifically, authorizers typically want their programs to be funded at high levels, but the appropriators get to make the final determination of a program's appropriations levels, irrespective of the program's authorization (e.g., Fenno 1966; LeLoup 1980; Schick 1995; Shuman 1992). Authorizing committees find it problematic that appropriators have the final say regarding the funding a program receives from year to year. The power of an authorizing committee is tied to an ability to shape and design the details of a program or agency. They also want to ensure that the program receives the funding necessary to achieve its goals. One way that authorizing committees have tried to have greater say in the appropriations process is by specifying funding levels in a short-term authorization. Authorization levels can be set as being "such sums as necessary," which delegates decisions about appropriate funding to appropriators, or it can be made a specific funding amount.

The authorization of appropriations can therefore be viewed as a signaling mechanism. The goal of including specific proposed funding levels in the authorization is to signal to appropriators, and to other policy actors, the funding levels that the authorizing committee thinks are appropriate for the program. Different types of authorizations send different types of signals. With a permanent authorization, the authorization committee is signaling that it does not desire to involve itself in the debate over funding for this activity; it is leaving funding decisions in the hands of the Appropriations Committees. With a specific short-term authorization, the authorizing committee is signaling to appropriators specific funding levels they desire for the program.

Signaling is necessary for authorizing committees because they generally cannot appropriate directly; they can only signal to appropriators the funding level they want a program to receive. Appropriators often work very hard to get around their inability to appropriate directly by passing mandatory spending programs (e.g., Weaver 1988). For example, the Transportation Equity Act for the 21st Century (TEA-21) created a process known as revenue aligned budget authority (RABA), whereby highway funding is tied to estimates of Highway Trust Fund receipts made when TEA-21 was enacted. RABA is designed to ensure that highway program funding tracks link with anticipated trust fund revenues, something that has not historically occurred.

Budget scholars have recognized the signaling purpose of short-term authorizations and the different signals sent by annual and multiyear authorizations (e.g., Fenno 1966; LeLoup 1980; Schick 1995; Shuman 1992; Wildavsky 1992). In the first case, authorizers want to be able to revisit annually the funding signal they are sending to appropriators. In the second case, the authorizing committee sends a series of signals regarding the specific funding trajectory they want for a program. By authorizing a program for only short periods, they can revisit and revise the signal they want to send regarding a program's appropriations levels. Additionally, the temporal closeness of an authorization and an appropriation is thought to improve the ability of an authorizing committee to influence appropriations decisions. Of course, authorizing committees use a variety of other techniques as part of the authorization process to influence appropriations, including earmarks for projects they deem important.

An additional benefit of the authorization-signaling model is that it allows authorizing committees to send signals to policy actors other than appropriators, especially constituents and interest groups. Because authorizing committees are generally populated with members who have a high demand for the committee's policy outputs (Shepsle 1978; cf. Krehbiel 1991), they have an incentive to authorize high levels of spending, as interest groups and their constituents would like. This strategy forces appropriators to make the tough choice to refuse to provide the total amount of funding authorized (Wildavsky 1992; Shuman 1992). Authorization committee members can therefore use authorization targets as a tool to inoculate themselves against criticism from the groups with which they work closely.

Recently, authorization committees have been sending a different sort of signal to appropriators by failing to renew the authorization of appropriations for many programs. Both House and Senate rules state that no appropriation shall be made for a program that does not have an authorization. If an unauthorized appropriation is proposed, any member can raise a point of order against the appropriation, although it is possible to waive these rules (Tiefer 1989, 966–72). When authorization committees fail to reauthorize a program, it can signal to appropriators that there is conflict among authorization committee members, or conflicts in Congress at large, about the efficacy of the program.

The bond between authorization committees and agencies is well known. Whether these are called iron triangles or something else, historically they link interests, agencies, and authorization committees in an effort to make the program effective. One means by which they gain power is by ensuring that they correctly inform their fellow members of Congress about the relative effectiveness of programs emerging from their jurisdiction (e.g., Krehbiel 1991). Thus, authorizing committees want programs to be funded at a level that will ensure successful implementation, as underfunding is a clear factor in implementation failures (e.g., Montjoy and O'Toole 1979). Short-term authorizations facilitate the work of committees in modifying a program so that it better addresses the concerns of Congress. Additionally, they provide new opportunities for members and interest groups alike to pressure appropriators regarding the appropriate funding levels for the program.

From the agency's perspective, reauthorizations present opportunities to make the case for why a given program is important and why it should receive higher funding levels. It also is an opportunity for agencies to energize the interest groups that are important supporters in their legislative efforts, especially since clientele support can be key to winning larger budgets from Congress (Berry 1989). An additional benefit of having greater resources is that it can help to ensure that Congress and others see the agency as being effective, which boosts its prestige and helps the agency avoid the harsh scrutiny that often accompanies implementation failures.

Competing Theories of Congressional Appropriations

When considered within the context of the congressional policy process, a signaling model based on short-term authorizations has a strong basis. Authorization committees spend a tremendous amount of time crafting reauthorization legislation—including the language authorizing appropriations—and authorization committee members, interest groups, and other interested actors often refer to a program's authorized funding levels when making the case for the appropriations amount it should receive. However, appropriators are not required to listen to these signals, and there are other factors that may influence their behavior. I consider three rival explanations for the spending decisions made by appropriators.

Incrementalism

There are many different definitions for incrementalism (e.g., Berry 1990). In budgeting, incrementalism can refer to a variety of budget-specific factors, such as failing to pay attention to the budgetary base, the regularity of the relationship among budget players, the narrowness of the bargaining between actors, or the smallness of the change in the budget. This analysis focuses on the size of the change, which Wanat (1978) has referred to as "descriptive incrementalism." This form of incrementalism examines changes in appropriations from one year to the next, focusing on whether the relative changes have been small from year to year. Under this conception, appropriators make appropriations decisions by adjusting spending upward or downward in small increments from the amount appropriated in the previous year. In this model there is signaling, but not from authorizers. Instead, appropriators look to their own work on the previous appropriation and use that funding level—and the level of change used in the past year—as a signal of how much appropriations should change in the current year.

Partisanship

Appropriations decisions can also be viewed through the lens of partisanship (e.g., Kiewiet and McCubbins 1991). This theory holds that each party has a unique position on appropriations that is ideologically dependent. Democrats are very approving of government activity, and therefore government spending. Republicans, being less supportive of the government and skeptical of its effectiveness, are not supportive of additional government spending either. Under this theory, government spending should increase at a faster rate when there is unified Democratic control of government compared to periods of divided government or unified Republican control. Because congressional dynamics are party based, especially in the House, it is possible for this partisan model to be implemented to influence the budget process (e.g., Cox and McCubbins 1993).

Institutional Control of Appropriations by Rules

Over the past twenty years, Congress has enacted several internal controls designed to rein in spending. The two most important enactments were the Gramm-Rudman-Hollings Act (GRH) and the 1990 Budget Enforcement Act (BEA), which was extended in 1997 and expired with the 2002 appropriations cycle. GRH was designed to control the deficit by setting yearly deficit targets. The BEA focused on limiting spending by placing caps on appropriations for various categories of discretionary spending. Discretionary spending was divided into three categories: defense, international, and domestic. For the years 1991–93, the caps were kept distinct, and appropriations limits were measured for each category separately. For the years 1993–94, the caps were aggregated, and discretionary spending was limited under this single cap. Since 1994, spending has been categorized as either defense or nondefense (Collender 1997, esp. 25–28). If these rules dominate the appropriations process, then regardless of the signaling that occurs, appropriators are constrained by the rules from listening to these signals.

Research Questions

These various theories can be tested in order to determine the importance of signaling by authorizing committees. If the signals used in authorization legislation influence the appropriations process, then it may solely explain why short-term authorizations are used. However, if these signals are not powerful, then one of the rival explanations may explain why this is the case. This analysis focuses on addressing three issues:

- Do authorizing committees authorize higher levels of spending than ultimately will be appropriated by the Appropriations Committee?
- Are the annual changes in appropriations for programs with short-term authorizations different from the changes in appropriations for programs with permanent authorizations?
- Will programs with expired short-term authorizations receive different funding consideration from the Appropriations Committee compared to programs with active short-term authorizations?

The hypotheses are tested using two related data sets. The first is composed of data for the fiscal years 1977–98 from four policy areas—commerce, defense, education, and transportation—as listed in table 4.1. Of the 562 cases included in this analysis, 280 (49.8 percent) had an active short-term authorization, 144 (25.6 percent) had an expired short-term authorization, and 138 (24.6 percent) had a "such sums as necessary" authorization. "Active authorizations" are those authorizations for which there is a specific authorization of appropriation for the fiscal year. If the authorization has lapsed, it is considered expired. "Such sums as necessary" language is a specific phrase used by authorizers when they do not want to specify funding levels for a program or an activity. The second data set covers a shorter time frame, fiscal years 1989–98. During this time, there was a sharp increase in the number of expired authorizations, and these data examine a broader policy cross-section, including agriculture, commerce, defense, education, international relations, and transportation, also shown in table 4.1. Of the 378 cases included in this analysis, 113 (32.0 percent) had an active short-term authorization, 117 (33.1 percent) had an expired short-term authorization, and 123 (34.8 percent) had a "such sums as necessary" authorization.

Table 4.1 Programs Examined in These Analyses

AGRICULTURE	EDUCATION
Animal and Plant Inspection Program	Corporation for Public Broadcasting*
Commodity Credit Corporation B Export Programs	Bilingual Education*
	Impact Aid*
Commodity Credit Corporation B Operations	Rehabilitation Services*
	Vocational Education*
Food Safety Inspection Program	National Endowment for the Arts*
Food Stamps	National Endowment for the Humanities*
Women, Infants, and Children Program	Pell Grants*
	Title I*[1]
COMMERCE	
	INTERNATIONAL RELATIONS
Commodity Futures Trading Commission*	
Consumer Product Safety Commission*	Arms Control and Disarmament Agency
Federal Communication Commission*	State Department B Administration of Foreign Affairs
Federal Trade Commission*	
Nuclear Regulatory Commission*	State Department B Funding for International Organizations
Securities and Exchange Commission*	
U.S. Travel and Trade Administration	Peace Corps
	U.S. AID
DEFENSE	U.S. Information Agency
Military Construction*	TRANSPORTATION
Naval Oil Reserves*	
Operation and Maintenance*	Amtrak*[1]
Personnel*	Appalachian Regional Commission*
Procurement*	Coast Guard*
Research and Development*	Federal Aviation Administration*
	Mass Transit*[1]
	National Highway Traffic Safety Administration*
	National Transportation Safety Board*

Note: Items marked with * appear in the FY 1977–98 data set.
[1]This program does not appear in the 1989–98 data set.

Enacted Appropriations Compared to Requests

If appropriators are paying attention to the funding requests from the authorizing committees, then there should be a close tracking between the specific program funding levels requested by authorizing committees and the funding appropriated to the program. This issue can be examined by computing the percentage difference between the levels authorized for each program with a short-term authorization and (a) the subsequent amount appropriated and (b) the budget authority granted to the program. Appropriations are the most common form of budget authority and provide legal authority for an agency to incur obligations and make payments from the treasury. However, budget authority can also be broader,

Table 4.2 The Difference between Authorizations and Appropriations, FY
       1977–1998

		Mean Difference	N
Fiscal Years 1977–98	Difference between Authorization and Appropriations	-5.57	295
	Difference between Authorization and Budget Authority	-3.91	295
	Defense Authorization Compared to Budget Authority	-2.12	91
	Nondefense Authorization Compared to Budget Authority	-4.71	204
Fiscal Years 1989–98	Difference between Authorization and Appropriations	-30.54	89
	Difference between Authorization and Budget Authority	-3.54	89
	Defense Authorization Compared to Budget Authority	-3.94	47
	Nondefense Authorization Compared to Budget Authority	-4.5%	42

allowing agencies to obligate and spend the proceeds of offsetting receipts, such as fees (Collender 1999, 196–97).

Table 4.2 shows the percentage difference between the levels authorized for each program with a short-term authorization and the subsequent amount appropriated using both the 1977–98 data set and the broader 1989–98 data set. From 1977 to 1998, the mean difference between authorizations and appropriations was 5.57 percent; the gap between authorizations and budget authority was slightly lower. From 1989 to 1998, the gap between authorizations and appropriations is much higher—30.5 percent—but the gap between authorizations and budget authority remains similar to that in earlier years, at 3.5 percent. The primary difference between budget authority and appropriations during this period is that appropriations data do not include unappropriated sources of budget authority available to independent regulatory agencies, such as revenues from fees, fines, and administrative penalties. Although the gap between authorizations and appropriations may seem high, they compare quite favorably to studies conducted by the U.S. Advisory Commission on Intergovernmental Relations (ACIR) during the Great Society. ACIR study found a 20 percent gap between authorizations and appropriations in 1965 and a 35 percent gap in 1970 (Schick 1995).

Table 4.3 Authorization-Appropriations Gaps by Presidential
            Administration

	Authorization -Appropriations Gap (%)		
	Mean	Median	N
Carter Administration	0.84	1.89	54
Reagan Administration	5.83	3.58	122
Bush Administration	1.64	4.27	46
Clinton Administration	4.42	6.04	73

Table 4.2 also shows that there is no significant difference between the budget authority allocated for defense and nondefense programs. The lack of difference between defense and nondefense programs is significant because defense functions are subject to annual authorizations, and the domestic programs included in this analysis are almost all subject to multiyear authorizations.[2] This suggests that there is little difference between the way in which multiyear and annual authorizations are treated in the appropriations process. It also suggests that defense and nondefense appropriations are treated differently in the authorization process, as the dollars are being doled out.

Table 4.3 shows a disturbing trend for authorizing committees. When the last four presidential terms are compared, the median gap between authorizations and appropriations has steadily risen. During the Carter Administration, the gap was less than 2 percent. By contrast, the median gap was more than 6 percent during first six years of the Clinton Administration. Over the intervening years, the gap between authorizations and appropriations steadily rose. This trend suggests that the signals sent by authorization committees to appropriators have become less effective over time, as other trends have come to the fore.

Are All Short-Term Authorizations Equal?

Before considering why the gap between authorizations and appropriations has grown over time, it is important to first determine if there is a difference in how various short-term authorizations are treated by appropriators. Authorizing committees can send three different types of signals to appropriators:

- They can authorize a short-term authorization with specific funding targets,
- They can pass a more permanent, "such sums as necessary" authorization, or

Table 4.4 Annual Percentage Change in Budget Authority and Appropriations for Programs with Different Authorization Statuses, FY 1976–1998

| | 1976–98 | | | | 1989–98 | | | |
| | Change in Budget Authority | | Change in Appropriations | | Change in Budget Authority | | Change in Appropriations | |
	Mean	Median	Mean	Median	Mean	Median	Mean	Median
Short-term, Expired Authorizations	7.87 (144)	2.04 (144)	5.93 (144)	3.63 (144)	1.99% (N = 105)	1.72 (N = 105)	-1.66% (N = 105)	0.00 (N = 105)
Short-term, Active Authorizations	9.20 (280)	2.74 (280)	8.64 (280)	2.43 (280)	2.68 (N = 102)	2.03 (N = 102)	1.17 (N = 102)	1.46 (N = 102)
Such Sums as Necessary@ Authorizations	6.62 (138)	4.89 (138)	6.48 (138)	4.90 (138)	14.68 (N = 103)	3.13 (N = 103)	14.73 (N = 103)	3.13 (N = 103)
ANOVA Between-Group Results	Sum of Squares	Mean Square	F	Sig.	Sum of Squares	Mean Square	F	Sig.
Annual Change in Budget Authority	0.064	0.032	0.081	0.922	10,513.7	5,356.9	1.56	0.233
Annual Change in Appropriations Levels	0.086	0.043	0.107	0.899	15,875.6	7,938	2.29	0.104

Note: The differences between these programs are similar whether all three types of programs are compared together in an ANOVA, or in two-way comparisons between active authorizations and either expired or permanent authorizations.

• They can fail to reauthorize a program, allowing it to operate with an expired authorization.

By comparing the percentage annual change in appropriations and in budget authority for each type of authorization, it is possible to determine if there is any difference between how appropriators treat different programs with different authorizations. Descriptive statistics and an analysis of variance (ANOVA) were used to test for differences among the three groups. Initial differences between authorization levels for different programs can be seen by comparing the mean and median annual change in appropriations and budget authority for each type of program. Table 4.4 shows the findings from these analyses for the years 1976–98 and 1989–98. In both cases, the analysis of variance examining the between group differences for the change in budget authority for the three programs shows that these differences are not statistically significant. The data show that the "such sums as necessary" cases always have the largest median change among the three programs. However, the mean growth for active short-term authorizations and expired authorizations vary over the two time frames. For the shorter time frame, expired authorizations have the lowest annual growth rate, but the active short-term authorizations fare worst in the longer time frame. The results of an ANOVA show that there is little statistical difference between the three types of authorizations. There is also no statistical difference between the growth rates for active and expired authorizations, with a difference of means test producing a statistical result of 0.475.

These data suggest that the way in which short-term authorizations are treated has changed over time, as the gap between authorizations and appropriations has grown over time. Additionally, there have been slight changes in the level of funding provided to programs with expired authorizations. However, the signaling mechanisms that are contained in authorizations are relatively weak. The lack of differentiation between how programs with varying authorization statuses—and thus various signaling strategies—are treated by appropriators suggests that during the period covered by this analysis, appropriators were using a different decision rule for determining program funding levels other than referencing the program's authorization status.

How Budget Rules Rule

If appropriators do not listen to the signals being sent by authorizers, what governs their decision-making? One alternative is that the budget process is merely incremental. The Historical Tables: Budget of the United States Government, Fiscal Year 2001 lists the annual changes in outlays for each fiscal year since 1962 for mandatory and discretionary spending. Figure 4.1 shows the annual percentage change in outlays for all domestic spending, for defense spending, and for all other domestic spending. Notice that there is a sizable variation from year to year in spending, especially when discretionary domestic and defense spending are considered separately. The standard deviation for all three categories of spending is relatively large—4.39 for all discretionary spending, 6.95 for defense spending, and 4.65 for domestic spending. The interquartile ranges for the same three categories are also large—7.16, 12.29, and 4.65 respectively for the three categories. The relatively wide variations suggest that, historically, appropriations decisions have not been purely incremental.

Figure 4.1 also highlights that the partisan explanation is less than satisfactory for explaining the changes in spending over time. Although annual changes in outlays were high during the Carter years, which were also a period of very high inflation, they were much lower during the first two years of the Clinton Administration. Additionally, over the last thirty-five years there have been relatively few periods of unified government, and partisanship has made the appropriations process more difficult.

Table 4.5 Changes in Discretionary Outlays under Various Budget
Rules

	N	Mean	Standard Deviation	Standard Error of Mean	Significance, Difference of Means t-test
BEA	10	2.16	2.96	0.94	
Other	13	7.51	3.90	1.08	0.00
Gramm-Rudman	5	3.79	1.86	0.83	
Other	18	5.57	4.83	1.14	0.22

Although there are differences between expenditures during the periods of unified Democratic control compared to the other periods, these differences are not significant.

Figure 4.1 also suggests that the full enforcement of the budget rules associated with the Budget Enforcement Act (BEA) is affecting the appropriations process. The BEA contained two "hammers." There were discretionary spending limits, or caps, that controlled the growth of the discretionary budget, and Pay-As-You-Go (PAYGO) rules, which required the net effect of all revenue and mandatory spending legislation to be revenue neutral. The spending caps were especially important because they limited spending at a fixed amount not tied to the deficit; neither increasing revenues nor lowering mandatory spending was allowed as a means of circumventing the caps (Collender 1999, 24–30).

Table 4.5 shows the effectiveness of rule-based appropriations efforts. Starting with Gramm-Rudman-Hollings, the overall growth in domestic discretionary spending was brought lower than it was historically, and the BEA lowered discretionary spending even more. House and Senate Appropriations Committee subcommittee chairmen were constrained by the Section 302(b) allocations they received. The appropriations bill that emerged from each subcommittee was required to fall within this allocation. With such constraints on appropriators, it is not surprising that there was such a sharp shift—as shown in table 4.3—in the gap between authorizations and appropriations over time. As the deficit rose and the Congress adopted new rules to constrain appropriations, the signaling mechanism contained within authorization legislation became less meaningful. The only way authorizers could make their funding authorizations stick was to have a mechanism to make their program funding mandatory, as the transportation committees did when creating the Revenue Aligned Budget Authority (RABA), which linked surface transportation spending to the funding contained within the transportation trust funds.

Figure 4.1 Outlays by Budget Enforcement Act Category, 1962–2009 (in billions of dollars)

Fiscal Year	Total Outlays	Discretionary				
			National Defense	Nondefense		
		Total		Total	International	Domestic
1962	106.8	72.1	52.6	19.5	5.5	14.0
1963	111.3	75.3	53.7	21.6	5.2	16.3
1964	118.5	79.1	55.0	24.1	4.6	19.5
1965	118.2	77.8	51.0	26.8	4.7	22.1
1966	134.5	90.1	59.0	31.1	5.1	26.1
1967	157.5	106.5	72.0	34.5	5.3	29.1
1968	178.1	118.0	82.2	35.8	4.9	31.0
1969	183.6	117.3	82.7	34.6	4.1	30.5
1970	195.6	120.3	81.9	38.3	4.0	34.4
1971	210.2	122.5	79.0	43.5	3.8	39.8
1972	230.7	128.5	79.3	49.2	4.6	44.6
1973	245.7	130.4	77.1	53.3	4.8	48.5
1974	269.4	138.2	80.7	57.5	6.2	51.3
1975	332.3	158.0	87.6	70.3	8.2	62.2
1976	371.8	175.6	89.9	85.7	7.5	78.2
TQ	96.0	48.1	22.3	25.7	3.3	22.4
1977	409.2	197.1	97.5	99.6	8.0	91.5
1978	458.7	218.7	104.6	114.1	8.5	105.5
1979	504.0	240.0	116.8	123.2	9.1	114.1
1980	590.9	276.3	134.6	141.7	12.8	128.9
1981	678.2	307.9	158.0	149.9	13.6	136.3
1982	745.7	326.0	185.9	140.0	12.9	127.1
1983	808.4	353.3	209.9	143.4	13.6	129.8
1984	851.9	379.4	228.0	151.4	16.3	135.1
1985	946.4	415.8	253.1	162.7	17.4	145.3
1986	990.4	438.5	273.8	164.7	17.7	147.0
1987	1,004.1	444.2	282.5	161.7	15.2	146.5
1988	1,064.5	464.4	290.9	173.5	15.7	157.8
1989	1,143.6	488.8	304.0	184.8	16.6	168.2
1990	1,253.2	500.6	300.1	200.4	19.1	181.4
1991	1,324.4	533.3	319.7	213.6	19.7	193.9
1992	1,381.7	533.8	302.6	231.2	19.2	212.1
1993	1,409.5	539.4	292.4	247.0	21.6	225.4
1994	1,461.9	541.4	282.3	259.1	20.8	238.3
1995	1,515.8	544.9	273.6	271.3	20.1	251.2
1996	1,560.5	532.7	266.0	266.7	18.3	248.4
1997	1,601.2	547.2	271.7	275.6	19.0	256.6
1998	1,652.6	552.1	270.2	281.9	18.1	263.8
1999	1,701.9	572.0	275.5	296.5	19.5	277.0
2000	1,788.8	614.8	295.0	319.9	21.3	298.6
2001	1,863.8	649.3	306.1	343.3	22.5	320.8
2002	2,011.0	734.3	348.9	385.4	26.2	359.2
2003	2,157.6	825.7	404.9	420.8	27.9	392.8
2004*	2,318.8	908.2	451.6	456.6	38.9	417.7
2005*	2,399.8	914.0	448.2	465.8	40.1	425.7
2006*	2,473.3	892.3	434.6	457.7	34.5	423.2
2007*	2,592.1	904.4	445.6	458.8	33.8	425.0
2008*	2,724.3	922.9	465.5	457.4	34.5	422.9
2009*	2,853.5	942.3	485.6	456.7	34.9	421.8

Figure 4.1 Continued

	Mandatory and Net Interest								
		Mandatory							
			Programmatic						
Fiscal Year	Total	Total	Total	Social Security	Deposit Insurance	Means Tested Entitlements[1]	Other	Undistributed Offsetting Receipts[2]	Net Interest
1962	34.7	27.9	33.1	14.0	-0.4	4.3	15.1	-5.3	6.9
1963	36.0	28.3	34.1	15.5	-0.4	4.7	14.3	-5.8	7.7
1964	39.4	31.2	36.9	16.2	-0.4	5.0	16.1	-5.7	8.2
1965	40.4	31.8	37.8	17.1	-0.4	5.2	15.8	-5.9	8.6
1966	44.4	35.0	41.5	20.3	-0.5	5.8	16.0	-6.5	9.4
1967	51.0	40.7	48.0	21.3	-0.4	6.2	20.9	-7.3	10.3
1968	60.2	49.1	57.1	23.3	-0.5	7.5	26.8	-8.0	11.1
1969	66.3	53.6	61.6	26.7	-0.6	8.6	26.9	-8.0	12.7
1970	75.4	61.0	69.6	29.6	-0.5	10.1	30.4	-8.6	14.4
1971	87.6	72.8	82.9	35.1	-0.4	13.4	34.8	-10.1	14.8
1972	102.1	86.7	96.2	39.4	-0.6	16.9	40.6	-9.6	15.5
1973	115.3	98.0	111.4	48.2	-0.8	16.7	47.3	-13.4	17.3
1974	131.1	109.7	126.4	55.0	-0.6	20.2	51.9	-16.7	21.4
1975	174.4	151.1	164.7	63.6	0.5	25.7	75.0	-13.6	23.2
1976	196.2	169.5	183.9	72.7	-0.6	30.5	81.3	-14.4	26.7
TQ	47.9	41.0	45.2	19.5	-0.1	7.6	18.2	-4.2	6.9
1977	212.1	182.2	197.1	83.7	-2.8	33.2	83.0	-14.9	29.9
1978	240.0	204.6	220.3	92.4	-1.0	35.2	93.7	-15.7	35.5
1979	264.0	221.4	238.9	102.6	-1.7	38.3	99.7	-17.5	42.6
1980	314.6	262.1	282.0	117.1	-0.4	45.0	120.4	-19.9	52.5
1981	370.3	301.6	329.6	137.9	-1.4	52.2	140.9	-28.0	68.8
1982	419.8	334.8	360.9	153.9	-2.1	52.2	156.8	-26.1	85.0
1983	455.0	365.2	399.2	168.5	-1.2	57.3	174.6	-34.0	89.8
1984	472.4	361.3	393.3	176.1	-0.8	58.6	159.4	-32.0	111.1
1985	530.6	401.1	433.8	186.4	-2.2	62.9	186.6	-32.7	129.5
1986	551.9	415.9	448.9	196.5	1.5	66.9	183.9	-33.0	136.0
1987	559.9	421.3	463.6	205.1	3.1	70.8	184.6	-42.3	138.6
1988	600.0	448.2	492.9	216.8	10.0	78.1	188.0	-44.7	151.8
1989	654.8	485.8	530.2	230.4	22.0	85.4	192.4	-44.3	169.0
1990	752.6	568.2	604.9	246.5	57.9	95.7	204.8	-36.7	184.3
1991	791.0	596.6	635.9	266.8	66.2	117.3	185.7	-39.4	194.4
1992	847.8	648.5	687.8	285.2	2.6	143.6	256.4	-39.3	199.3
1993	870.1	671.4	708.7	302.0	-28.0	159.1	275.7	-37.4	198.7
1994	920.5	717.5	755.3	316.9	-7.6	173.4	272.6	-37.8	202.9
1995	970.9	738.8	783.3	333.3	-17.9	184.8	283.1	-44.5	232.1
1996	1,027.8	786.8	824.4	347.1	-8.4	191.0	294.7	-37.6	241.1
1997	1,054.0	810.0	860.0	362.3	-14.4	198.0	314.1	-50.0	244.0
1998	1,100.5	859.4	906.6	376.1	-4.4	204.8	330.0	-47.2	241.1
1999	1,129.9	900.1	940.6	387.0	-5.3	217.0	341.8	-40.4	229.8
2000	1,173.9	951.0	993.6	406.0	-3.1	232.6	358.0	-42.6	223.0
2001	1,214.4	1,008.3	1,055.3	429.4	-1.4	248.1	379.2	-47.0	206.2
2002	1,276.6	1,105.7	1,153.1	452.1	-1.0	280.8	421.2	-47.4	171.0
2003	1,331.9	1,178.9	1,233.2	470.5	-1.4	306.7	457.5	-54.4	153.1
2004*	1,410.7	1,254.4	1,313.7	492.0	-1.5	331.7	491.5	-59.3	156.3
2005*	1,485.8	1,307.9	1,371.0	510.5	-1.5	347.1	515.0	-63.1	177.9
2006*	1,581.0	1,367.6	1,445.0	529.1	-1.0	357.8	559.1	-77.4	213.4
2007*	1,687.7	1,441.5	1,520.3	551.8	-1.2	371.9	597.8	-78.9	246.2
2008*	1,801.3	1,526.7	1,602.7	576.3	-1.9	396.0	632.2	-76.0	274.6
2009*	1,911.1	1,612.0	1,692.1	607.8	-2.0	419.1	667.2	-80.2	299.1

[1]Includes Medicaid, food stamps, family support assistance (AFDC), supplemental security income (SSI), child nutrition programs, refundable portions of earned income tax credits (EITC and HITC) and child tax credit, welfare contingency fund, child care entitlement to States, temporary assistance to needy families, foster care and adoption assistance, State children's health insurance and veterans' pensions.
[2]Including asset sales.
*Estimates

Summary

Short-term authorizations are designed to serve as a mechanism by which authorizing committees can signal to the Appropriations Committee the appropriate funding level for a specific program. However, the power of the authorization signal has been declining over the past three decades. The gap between authorizations and appropriations has become larger over time, with the median gap rising from less than 2 percent in the Carter Administration to more than 6 percent during the Clinton Administration. In the 1960s, the ACIR explained the gap between authorizations and appropriations by arguing that Congress was pressured to divert funding to the Vietnam War (Schick 1995, 176). It would be easy to argue that, in recent years, Congress has been under similar pressure to lower deficits and constrain spending. However, examining historical data on budget outlays shows that it was the implementation of specific rules to control spending—first Gramm-Rudman-Hollings, then the Budget Enforcement Act—that created an environment in which discretionary spending was highly constrained. Appropriators do not have the same capacity to meet the demands of authorizers or the interests who lobby for a given program to receive appropriations equal to the amounts authorized.

In recent years, authorization committees have also changed the policy environment somewhat with a sharp increase in the number of programs operating with an expired authorization. Since the CBO began collecting data on unauthorized appropriations in 1985, the number of programs operating with an expired authorization has grown steadily. The programs with expired authorizations have historically been politically contentious, and although both House and Senate rules suggest that allowing a program's authorization to expire would be problematic, the reality is that a program's funding continues to grow at roughly the same rate after it expires. When a policy is difficult to address, an authorizing committee can allow the program's authorization to expire without being concerned that program will be terminated. It may be that these programs would likely receive less funding than their authorized levels but for the fact that these expired programs no longer have authorized levels of spending.

5

Oversight and Short-Term Authorizations

When members of Congress create new programs, they want to control how the program is implemented. Congress generally does this through *ex post* or *ex ante* controls over agency behavior. Ex ante controls attempt to limit or to influence agency choices prior to a final action being taken. McCubbins (1985) notes that when an agency is designed, ex ante controls are created. These controls can include limiting the scope of an agency's activities, the implementation tools (e.g., direct provision of a good versus contracting) they can use in meeting their goals, and the settings in which regulatory activities can occur. Ex post controls attempt to limit or influence an agency after the agency has already taken action. Congressional committee oversight hearings are an example of an ex post control mechanism; these hearings allow the committee to pressure an agency regarding how it is acting with regard to a given policy or program.

Short-term authorizations have attributes that can promote and facilitate both ex post and ex ante controls. First, the substantive component of the legislation structures a program's operations so that it will be implemented in the manner that the committee desires. When crafting this substantive language, a committee uses its powers to constrain agencies so that they will behave in the manner that the committee prefers (e.g., McCubbins 1985; McCubbins, Noll, and Weingast 1987; Moe 1984; Weingast 1984). Congress can inhibit certain agency behaviors and promote others, depending on how the agency is structured and what powers the agency is given in its authorization. For example, Hammond (1986) provides a theoretical argument regarding how different agency structures can result in different policy outcomes than would result if the agency were organized in a different manner. In an example of this in practice, Cook (1989) notes that the Congress would not allow President Reagan to reorganize the Environmental Protection Agency because it felt that the way in which the agency was to be reorganized would markedly affect the agency's policy outcomes.

Second, when an authorization is short-term, it can provide Congress with enhanced control over a program because the expired authorization commits an authorizing committee to review the funding and operation of the program in the future (e.g., Aberbach 1990; Fisher 1983, 1979; Oleszek 1989; Schick 1995, 1983, 1980; Shuman 1992; Tiefer 1989). Annual and multiyear authorizations force policy committees to review a program or agency at a specific time. During the reauthorization process, interest groups and agency stakeholders have the opportunity to bring to the authorization committee concerns that they have about how the program or agency is operating. The committee also has an opportunity to adjust the underlying authorizing legislation, forcing the stakeholders implementing the program to respond in a different manner.

The next two chapters examine how short-term authorizations facilitate both ex post and ex ante forms of oversight. In this chapter, I examine the history of congressional oversight and put the oversight aspects of short-term authorizations into a historical context. I then show the limitations that exist in viewing short-term authorizations as a trigger for oversight but instead show how oversight is an ongoing process. Then, in chapter 6, I illustrate the way in which short-term authorizations facilitate ex ante control over policy, allowing Congress to "steer" the activities of agencies.

Congressional Oversight of Executive Agencies: A Brief History

Congress began to exercise its oversight capabilities in the early years of the Republic. The Federalists who preceded Jefferson believed in a strong executive and a strong federal government. They worked assiduously to achieve their goal of a strong government with a strong executive, and during the first two presidential administrations the executive branch dominated the legislative branch (Aberbach 1990; Schick 1983; White 1948). However, the period of executive dominance did not last a year into the nineteenth century. The Jeffersonians encouraged Congress to scrutinize the activities of the executive branch more carefully. One clear manifestation of this increased control was that Congress exercised more oversight over appropriations to executive agencies, making them much more detailed (White 1951). Scholars generally argue that the desire for a legislative branch stronger than the executive branch was the reality until the New Deal (e.g., White 1951). Schick (1983, 157–58) notes that:

Congress initiated and drafted most legislation . . . and it often legislated in great detail. Individual positions and their salaries were itemized in law; post roads were plotted by Congress. . . . . Congress could penetrate at will to the smallest administrative detail, giving the affected agency no course other than to follow its dictates.

By the late 1800s, the federal government had changed, as had opinions regarding the need for congressional control of the executive. From 1870 to 1880, the number of federal employees increased from 50,000 to 100,000. By the 1920s, civilian government employment had increased to the point that there were 550,000 workers on the government payroll (Schick 1983, 158). With so many federal workers and positions, it was no longer possible for Congress to be as meticulous in its control over every item in the budget. Issues and details that had previously been itemized in the federal budget were lumped together. The increased size of the federal bureaucracy required Congress to give away some of the control it previously had been able to exercise through the budget process. Also, during this same time, there was a tremendous growth in the regulatory capacities of the federal government and the complexity of the demands on the government. From roughly 1880 to 1920, the federal bureaucracy was expanded and institutionalized. This period saw the birth of the independent regulatory agency, and an evolution toward an administrative state (Carpenter 2001; Skowronek 1982).

In response to the new administrative complexity, Congress was forced to develop new processes and procedures. One solution to the problem was to delegate more decisions to executive agencies. For instance, after more than a century of setting tariff rates, the Congress delegated authority over setting tariff rates to the president in 1934 (Schick 1983). Congress also delegated more budget powers to the president, in an effort to strengthen congressional efforts to control agencies. With the creation of the Bureau of the Budget, the Congress empowered the president to control rogue agencies that were expanding rapidly. In essence, the Congress empowered the president to make an initial effort to control agencies—to constrain and to coordinate their budget requests—before Congress had to consider these budgetary matters. Until the end of World War II, the primary focal point for congressional oversight was the appropriations process. However, as a part of the 1946 Legislative Reorganization Act, Congress called on its committees to "exercise continuous watchfulness of the execution . . . of any laws . . . by the agencies in the executive branch of the Government" (Aberbach 1990; see also Galloway 1951).[1] Congress reiterated its desire to see committees perform effective oversight in 1971, when it amended the 1946 Act (Aberbach 1979). These efforts were designed to build the capacities within Congress for committees to conduct oversight. More staff, requirements for committees to develop oversight plans, and the creation of committees within Congress that are designed almost exclusively to conduct oversight all illustrate how these laws were intended to facilitate the oversight process (e.g., Aberbach 1990; Salisbury and Shepsle 1981).

Although Congress acted several times to promote committee oversight of agency activities, many scholars of the oversight process have argued that Congress has not fulfilled its mandate to perform "continuous watchfulness" (e.g., Aberbach 1979; Dodd and Schott 1979; Ogul 1976; Scher 1963). It is Ethridge's (1984) contention that scholars who view Congress as failing in its oversight activities make this argument because they see both a lack of incentives and political barriers to carrying out oversight activities. One argument is that oversight is not conducted because committees lack the time to do so. Lawmakers would rather engage in lawmaking than oversight, because lawmaking more effectively leads to the achievement of their reelection goal (e.g., Ogul 1976). In fact, oversight can antagonize agencies and impede their ability to get their constituent service requests met, which is also critical for members seeking reelection (Ethridge 1984; Fiorina 1977). A second argument is that authorizing committees dislike oversight because it can undermine support for programs under their jurisdiction and anger interest groups who are key constituents to committee members. Thus, special oversight committees, such as the House Government Reform and Oversight Committee, are often pressured by authorizing committees to avoid topics that would create problems for the authorizers (Dodd and Schott 1976; Ethridge 1984).

The view that Congress does not conduct effective oversight is undermined by data showing that the amount of oversight Congress conducts has increased dramatically over time. From the early 1960s to the mid-1980s, the number of days of oversight conducted by congressional committees increased by more than 300 percent. Oversight went from being less than one-tenth of the workload for congressional committees to being more than one-quarter of all activity. Likewise, during this period the number of bills passed by Congress declined markedly as the amount of oversight increased dramatically (Aberbach 1990, 34–39). Additionally, it should not be forgotten that one of the most effective means of conducting oversight is to legislate. As McCubbins (1985) notes, legislation allows Congress to place controls on the implementation mechanisms available to agencies. Congress can delegate powers through legislation or rein in powers that agencies have acquired.

Short-Term Authorizations and Oversight in the Modern Congress

Why has oversight increased so dramatically since the early 1960s? Committee staff explain the increase by suggesting that the government is more complex now than it was in the past, and therefore requires greater oversight. Of course, there is more staff, better staff, and more support from attached legislative organizations, such as the General Accounting Office, Congressional Budget Office, and Congressional Research Service, which are all directly accountable to Congress and can facilitate oversight activities (Aberbach 1990, chap. 2). However, members of Congress state that—except for scandals (agency malfeasance) or a severe policy crisis—the expiration of a short-term authorization is the most likely way in which a program will be added to the oversight agenda (Aberbach 1990, 109–20). Because Congress uses short-term authorizations more often today than in the past, the expiration of a program's authorization typically leads to oversight hearings. For example, the House and Senate Armed Services Committees conduct numerous oversight hearings annually as a part of the Department of Defense authorization. Likewise, the House and Senate Commerce Committees have dozens of independent regulatory agencies under their jurisdiction; many of these programs have very short authorizations, which means that some number of reauthorizations are always on the committee's agenda.

Of course, the need to reauthorize programs is not the only reason for oversight hearings. Aberbach (1990, 109–18) finds that clientele complaints are an important reason why committees hold oversight hearings, although not the highest rated reason. Interest groups and other parties affected by agency decision making often request oversight to inform committees about concerns they have regarding the implementation of a program. One interesting part of Aberbach's findings is that when a factor analysis is conducted regarding how issues get on the oversight agenda, clientele complaints cluster with general public concerns and district concerns. This suggests the possibility that either (a) interest groups are very effective at reflecting the concerns of their members, or (b) interest groups are very effective at creating grassroots support for the issues of greatest concern to them. There is clear evidence that there has been a dramatic growth in the use of grassroots lobbying by interest groups (Faucheaux 1995; P. H. Stone 1997), and groups may be using this lobbying tactic to bring problematic policies to the attention of members in order to encourage greater oversight.

Timing and Types of Oversight Hearings

There are different types of oversight hearings that congressional committees can conduct. The first type is referred to as police patrol oversight, in
which members of Congress systematically review the effectiveness of programs and agencies. Although these scholars generally argue that this type
of oversight does not occur often because it is inefficient, Aberbach's
(1990) data suggest that for most programs and agencies, police patrol
oversight is actually relatively common. One reason this type of hearing is
common is that short-term authorizations, which are designed to foster
systematic program review, are common.

Except in the case of the few programs that have an annual authorization, quite a bit of time can pass between authorizations. During these
intervening periods, problems may occur with the function of a program,
or interest groups may become concerned with the way in which an agency
is implementing the program. In such cases, groups may complain to the
committee of jurisdiction, requesting that the operations of the program
be investigated. This interest induced form of oversight is often referred to
as fire alarm oversight. The fire alarm is sounded when interest groups or
other constituents think that the agency has acted outside of its legal mandate, or groups have interpreted the mandate to mean something different
(Epstein and O'Halloran 1996; McCubbins and Schwartz 1984). Congress
can then determine if it should hold oversight hearings or otherwise inter-
vene in order to rein in the agency.

Scholars who advance the police patrol versus fire alarm theory suggest
that fire alarm oversight should be prominent and more common than
police patrol oversight, as fire alarm oversight is less costly. However, data
show that oversight is more common than is typically acknowledged, and
short-term authorizations, which can trigger police patrol oversight, are
quite common (e.g., Aberbach 1990). Furthermore, the literature on agendas (e.g., Kingdon 1995) suggest that once Congress has addressed a policy
question, it is unlikely to revisit the issue unless the "policy window" reopens
because of a crisis or scandal. Interest groups, especially those who were on
the losing end of the last policy debate, obviously have an incentive to try to
shape the debate in a way that benefits them before the policy window opens
again. Oversight hearings can be one way of accomplishing this goal.

Oversight and Short-Term Authorizations: The Case of Defense

The process of making defense policy is one in which the importance of
short-term authorizations can be seen over time. As I noted in chapter 2,

beginning in fiscal year 1960, the Senate Armed Services Committee required that an annual authorization be passed before appropriations could be made for the procurement of aircraft, missiles, and naval vessels because Congress wanted to exert more control over the way in which defense policy was made. Since then, nine other legislative enactments have required other components of the defense budget to undergo an annual authorization (Art 1985). By 1970, all weapons systems were subject to a short-term authorization, and the most recent major change was in 1982, when the Operations and Maintenance Account was brought under the annual defense authorization.

Does having almost the entirety of activities within the Department of Defense subject to short-term authorization facilitate quality oversight? The results are mixed. Art (1985) notes that the volume of report language issued by the Armed Services Committees grew rapidly from the 1960s through the 1980s. However, he also found that this work by the policy committee with jurisdiction over defense has mainly focused on authorizing specific systems through procurement, research, and development and not on examining how these various systems fit into an overall defense strategy. As Senator Sam Nunn (D-GA) explains:

> The budget cycle drives the Congress, and the Congress drives the executive branch to such an obsession that we don't have time to think about strategy. We never had a strategy hearing since I've been in the Senate.[2]

Senator Nunn's concerns are reflected by his colleagues in the House, one of whom said, "We don't talk about strategy or tactics to my satisfaction. . . . [W]e should be concerned with a proper defense policy and its match with our foreign policy" (Art 1985, 235). Some scholars (e.g., Art 1989) have proposed biennial budgeting for defense policy to improve opportunities for planning and to facilitate more effective defense oversight.

One attribute that has surfaced from placing most defense programs under the annual defense authorization is that defense oversight has been routinized. Most hearings that occur in the Armed Services Committees are related to the defense authorization; few are event driven (Balla and Deering 2001). For instance, in 1995, only three of twenty-one hearings held by the Senate Armed Services Committee were related to a specific military event, such as the conflict in Bosnia or the nuclear weapons threat in North Korea. Steven Balla and Chris Deering (2001) examine defense oversight in the 100th and 104th Congresses and find that more than 80 percent of all defense oversight in both the House and Senate Armed Services Committees is what can typically be referred to as police patrol oversight. This should not be surprising; with the annual defense authorization dominating the committees' agenda, they have little time to consider other issues (Art 1985, 1989).

This analysis demonstrates the type of oversight that occurs in the defense policy area under annual authorization. The annual nature of the defense authorization creates the environment for police patrol oversight because the committee is examining one issue in great detail year in and year out. Other data in the Balla and Deering analysis examining overall levels of oversight in other committees suggest that there is much more police patrol oversight in Congress than is traditionally thought. For these other committees, which typically will have agendas consisting almost entirely of programs with multi-year authorizations, it is not possible to know if there is any link between the levels and timing of police patrol or fire alarm oversight and the timing of the expiration of a program's authorization because their study does not specifically test that hypothesis. For the annual defense policy, however, the oversight environment is clearly dominated by police patrols.

Research Questions

The previous discussion suggests that short-term authorizations cause several important changes in the oversight-hearing environment. The following research questions are drawn from the literature discussed above.

- Does the expiration of a program's authorization cause the authorizing committee to hold hearings?
- At these hearings, does Congress hear from interest groups and agency stakeholders that represent a broad spectrum of interests?
- Between authorizations, will there be a limited amount of fire alarm oversight that will be triggered by interest groups or programmatic crises?
- Will programs with an expired authorization be subject to greater oversight scrutiny than will programs that are reauthorized in a timely manner?

If a short-term authorization is designed to facilitate oversight, then the reauthorization process and the holding of hearings should be roughly concomitant. A program with a short-term authorization should receive close scrutiny when the authorization is about to expire, as interest groups from both sides want to weigh in on how effectively the program is functioning, and the committee will want to have that information so it can make better decisions. Similarly, committees are expected to hold fire alarm hearings between authorizations as problems arise in order to be responsive to interest groups operating in their jurisdiction. Finally, the failure of a committee to reauthorize a program strongly suggests that the policy in question is controversial and that there is division within the committee (or between the committee and the floor) regarding what the correct policy is in this area. Therefore, it is expected that a program with an expired authorization will be subject to oversight hearings from two fronts. First, interest groups will want hearings to express support for or opposition to the existing policy. Second, the committee will hold hearings to discuss alternative legislative options in this area.

Analyzing Oversight

The data used to analyze oversight come from several sources. First, data from the Agendas Project can be used to identify all of the hearings for a specific program and the attributes of those hearings. Second, using this same data source, it is possible to reference the *CIS/Annual: Abstracts of Congressional Documents* and identify the witnesses who testify before Congress. The summaries of the hearings that come from the Agenda's Project data on hearings can also be used to determine if a hearing should be coded as a police patrol or fire alarm hearing. Balla and Deering (2001) identify six criteria that can be used to determine into which category a hearing falls. The criteria for fire alarm hearings include: (*a*) if the hearing is time proximate to a specific event; (*b*) if the hearing is in response to a very specific problem or event; and (*c*) if the hearing calls specific individuals to account for specific events. Without time proximity to a specific event, a hearing is considered a police patrol. These hearing data can then be combined with data on a program's authorization status using the U.S. Code, Congressional and Administrative News (USCCAN). The annual USCCAN volumes contain actual legislation, from which authorization data can be obtained.[3]

These hypotheses are tested on data from four policy areas: education, transportation, regulatory, and Social Security. The data are analyzed by program type and program. Table 5.1 shows the specific programs from each policy area that are included in the analysis. The hypotheses are tested using two different data sets. One uses the year as the unit of analysis and examines hearings by program by year, and the other uses the hearing as a unit of analysis and examines each hearing by program.

As the first research question notes, short-term authorizations should facilitate oversight. When examining hearings by program type, however, this becomes a questionable hypothesis. Consider three programs and the distribution of hearings across years where authorizations are permanent, short-term, or expired. Figure 5.1 shows the distribution of hearings by

Table 5.1 Programs Included in the Analysis of Oversight

EDUCATION
Disability Education
Head Start
National Endowment for the Arts
Vocational Education

REGULATORY
Commodity Futures Trading Commission
Consumer Product Safety Commission
Nuclear Regulat ory Commission
Securities and Exchange Commission

TRANSPORTATION
Amtrak
Coast Guard
Federal Aviation Administration
Mass Transit

SOCIAL SECURITY
Social Security

year for Social Security, a program with a permanent authorization. The number of hearings held each year varies widely, and there is little correlation between hearings held and other factors, such as media coverage of the issue or divided control of government.

Programs with short-term authorizations have similar hearing patterns, and these patterns do not seem to change even when the committee's authorization patterns change. The Coast Guard provides an interesting example in this regard. The program had an annual authorization until the early 1980s, when it then switched to a two-year authorization. Figure 5.2 shows that when the Coast Guard had an annual authorization, the committee alternated between having one hearing in one year, then two or three hearings the next. Once the Coast Guard authorization became a two-year authorization, the alternating hearing levels remained; just the volume changed, with the committee vacillating between holding two hearings in a year, followed by a year with three or four hearings. When the committee went to the two-year authorization, the off year was the year in which more hearings were held, suggesting a slight lag effect between hearings and legislative activity.

The expiration of a short-term authorization also does not necessarily mean that hearing patterns change dramatically. Consider the case of the Nuclear Regulatory Commission. Figure 5.3 shows the number of hearings held after the program's authorization expired, first in 1980, and then in 1985. After the extremely large number of hearings held in 1979 in the wake of the incident at the Three Mile Island nuclear power facility, the number of hearings held on the issue stayed within a range between ten and

Figure 5.1 The Number of Hearings Held per Year Regarding Social
Security

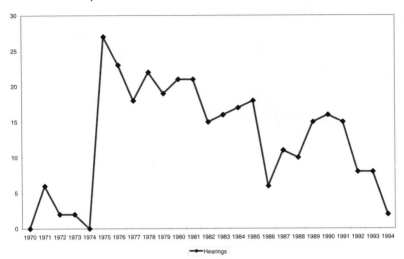

Figure 5.2 The Number of Hearings Held per Year Regarding the Coast
Guard and the Authorization Status of the Program

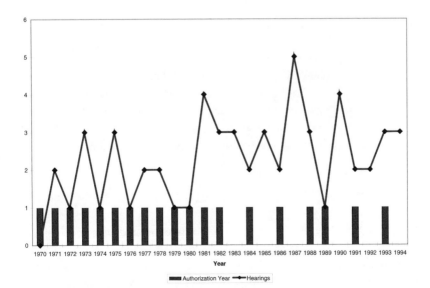

66   Chapter 5

Figure 5.3 The Number of Hearings Held per Year Regarding the Nuclear
          Regulatory Commission and the Authorization Status of the
          Program

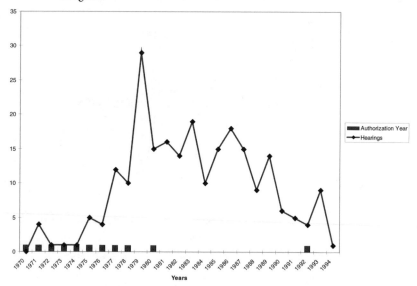

twenty through the 1980s, dropped to between five and ten in the early
1990s, and then dropped almost to one by 1994.

The three figures illustrate that there is no clear pattern of when Congress
will or will not hold hearings. If short-term authorizations are designed to
facilitate oversight, there should be some correlation between hearings held
and authorization years. Table 5.2 presents the correlations between hearing
activity and the expiration of authorizations and of media coverage. When
considering the correlation between hearings and other factors for each program type, the data show that hearings do not directly correlate with any of
the factors. It is not as though committees wait for an authorization to expire
to conduct hearings, nor do they hold hearings in a manner that is easily
modeled. A multivariate analysis confirms this finding; there is no clear relationship between hearings and the factors included in table 5.2.

Who Testifies?

Although it is difficult to predict the patterns associated with hearings, the
actual composition of any given hearing is relatively easy to predict.
Overall, the composition of hearings tends to be relatively similar across
hearing types. The *CIS Abstracts* lists the witnesses that appear before

Table 5.2 Correlations of Factors Related to the Number of Hearings Held, by Policy Area

	Education	Transportation	Regulatory	Social Security
Authorization Year	0.01 (0.96)	-0.13 (0.19)	-0.05 (0.70)	—
Previous Authorization Year	-0.01 (0.98)	-0.18 (0.08)	0.10 (0.31)	—
Expired Authorization	-0.06 (0.56)	0.5 (0.66)	-0.14 (0.20)	—
Number of Stories	0.02 (0.83)	0.77** (0.00)	0.35 (.0.00)	0.36 (0.08)
Unified Government	0.07 (0.43)	0.02 (0.87)	0.04 (0.67)	0.17 (0.43)
Divided Congress	-0.30** (0.00)	-0.02 (0.84)	-0.14 (0.15)	0.20 (0.33)
N	100	100	100	25

Note: Each cell contains the correlation coefficient and the statistical significance (in parentheses).
**Significant at the 0.05 level

Congress at each hearing, and it is possible to classify these individuals into categories. Wright (1996, chap. 2) provides a basic typology for classifying political interest groups, and five of the six types he identifies are used in this analysis: trade and professional associations, citizens groups, corporations, labor unions, and state/local governmental organizations. I then supplemented that list with three other types of witnesses that appear frequently before Congress: federal agencies, members of Congress, and congressional staff, including representatives of the General Accounting Office or the Congressional Budget Office.

The witnesses who testify at hearings reflect in part the desire of various policy stakeholders to participate in the political process regarding a specific topic, but also reflect the interest on the part of committee members and staff to hear specific viewpoints at a given hearing on a given topic. Even if a policy stakeholder wants to participate in a hearing, it is the prerogative of the committee to determine if this stakeholder can or cannot participate. Testifying is a key aspect of the work of interest groups (Schlozman and Tierney 1983), especially because of the role that it plays in conveying information to members. Hearings allow political stakeholders to provide political information to members (Ainsworth 1993), and this political information may be very helpful to off-committee members (Diermeier and Federsen 2000).

As figures 5.1, 5.2, and 5.3 show, Congress holds hearings frequently. However, it may be that the mix of voices it wants to hear varies between authorization years and off years, or between police patrol hearings and fire alarm hearings. For example, Congress might want to hear the views of practitioners between authorizations, as it assesses how programs are functioning, but might want to hear the views of executive agencies during the actual authorization debates. Similarly, fire alarm hearings might be a preferred time to request testimony from agency personnel, who have allowed some crisis to occur.

Before presenting data on the frequency of appearance of various witnesses before committees, it is first beneficial to discuss the relative frequency of authorization hearings compared with off-year hearings, and the number of police patrol hearings compared with the number of fire alarm hearings. In this analysis, approximately one-third of all hearings are held in an authorization year, and the frequency of police patrol and fire alarm hearings is similar to the results obtained by Balla and Deering (2001). The congressional hearing process is dominated by police patrol hearings; only 11 percent of all hearings were fire alarm hearings. Finally, approximately 70 percent of fire alarm hearings occurred in off years. The cases of fire alarm hearings during authorization years generally came from two sources of conflict. First, the Reagan budget of 1981 sparked hearings about how programs would be harmed by the proposed reconciliation legislation. Second, the National Endowment for the Arts sparked several fire alarm hearings over allegations that the NEA funded obscene art.

As one policy player, who worked in education policy for more than a decade, noted:

> Only a quarter of oversight actually examines the policy related specifically to programs. Most hearings focus on overall agency performance, financial oversight, appropriations, or the dreaded hearing on some fraud, waste, or abuse. The latter type of hearing is rare, but when they happen, they are so big. They require a tremendous amount of preparation time because we all have to think through the testimony strategically—what did we do about the problem, how rare is the problem, why is it not our fault, how will we ensure it never happens again.

Table 5.3 shows the distribution of witnesses for authorization years compared with off years. All hearings tend to have approximately twelve witnesses and last approximately two days, with hearings in both authorization years and off years being of similar length. Hearings tend to be dominated

Table 5.3 Witness Variation between Authorization and Off Years, by Program, 1970–1994

Witness Type	Authorization Status	All Programs	Transportation	Regulatory	Education
Mean Number of Witnesses	Off-Year	12.93	13.95	10.01	16.1
	Auth. Year	12.5	13.23	8.68	14.85
Agency Percent	Off-Year	2.39	2.41**	3.45	0.93
	Auth. Year	2.61	3.54**	2.77	0.88
Trade Percent	Off-Year	3.47	3.58	2.65	4.49
	Auth. Year	3.78	3.79	1.9	5.52
Citizen Percent	Off-Year	3.27	1.48	1.19	7.54
	Auth. Year	2.43	1.32	1.13	5.55
Inter-govt Percent	Off-Year	1.81	3.67**	0.22	2.49
	Auth. Year	1.37	1.73**	0.1	1.94
Labor Percent	Off-Year	0.31	0.69*	0.06	0.35
	Auth. Year	0.24	0.34*	0.03	0.27
Corporate Percent	Off-Year	1.08	0.84	1.99	0.01
	Auth. Year	1.17	1.2	2.35	0
Congress Member Percent	Off-Year	0.5	1.19	0.35	0.16
	Auth. Year	0.78	1.2	0.29	0.52
Congressional Staff Percent	Off-Year	0.11	0.09	0.09	0.14
	Auth. Year	0.13	0.13	0.1	0.18
N	Off-Year	253	64	109	80
	Auth. Year	120	56	31	33
Total Hearing Days	Off-Year	1.99	2.13	1.75*	2.25
	Auth. Year	2.02	2.05	2.05*	1.85

* Correlation is significant at the 0.10 level (2-tailed).
** Correlation is significant at the 0.05 level (2-tailed).

by agency personnel, trade associations, and citizen groups, with each of these groups having between two and four witnesses per hearing. All other groups constitute a small part of the hearings process, rarely having more than one witness per hearing. The only policy area that shows great differences in witness composition between authorization years and off years is transportation policy. For this policy area, agency personnel become a much more dominant force in authorization years, at the expense of intergovernmental representatives, who have more dominance in off years.

Table 5.4 Witness Variations between Police Patrol and Fire Alarm
        Hearings, by Program, 1970–1994

Witness Type		All Programs	Transportation	Regulatory	Education
Total Number of Witnesses	Police	12.99	13.44	9.92	16
	Fire	11.11	17	8.64	13
Agency Witnesses	Police	2.36*	2.89	3.13	0.89
	Fire	3.32*	3.67	4.23	1.1
Trade Witnesses	Police	3.73**	3.68	2.72	4.96*
	Fire	2.08**	3.67	1.23	3.00*
Citizen Witnesses	Police	3.07	1.43	1.30**	6.93
	Fire	2.37	1	0.55**	7.2
Inter-Govt Witnesses	Police	1.18	4	0.23	1.6
	Fire	1.72	2.7	0.19	2.4
Labor Witnesses	Police	0.28	0.43	0.06	0.36
	Fire	0.39	2.33	0.05	0
Corporate Witnesses	Police	1.08	0.99	2.11	0.01
	Fire	1.29	1.33	1.86	0
Congress Member Witnesses	Police	0.61	1.2	0.33	0.28
	Fire	0.39	1	0.36	0.1
Congressional Staff Witnesses	Police	0.12	0.11	0.08	0.17**
	Fire	0.08	0	0.14	0.00**
N	Police	335	114	118	103
	Fire	38	6	22	10
Total Hearing Days	Police	2.30*	2.42	2.3	2.16
	Fire	1.92*	2	1.91	1.9

* Correlation is significant at the 0.10 level (2-tailed).
** Correlation is significant at the 0.05 level (2-tailed).

The examination of police patrol and fire alarm hearings is slightly more difficult because of the dominance of police patrol hearings in the process. However, some basic trends can be seen in the data presented in table 5.4. There are differences in the length of the hearings, with police patrol hearings being longer than fire alarm hearings. Fire alarm hearings tend to focus on a very specific topic and tend to have slightly fewer witnesses—approximately two fewer—than police patrol hearings, which likely accounts for the shorter hearing time. There is also one important difference in the composition of witnesses between the two types of hearings. Agency personnel are more likely to be brought before a congressional committee at a fire alarm hearing, and trade witnesses are less likely to testify at a fire alarm hearing. This witness dynamic fits one classic presentation of a hearing, where a congressional committee brings a recalcitrant agency head before them—or the head of the agency who has some responsibility over a policy area where there has been a terrible tragedy—and ruthlessly questions the witness about the agency's malfeasance.

A final point about fire alarm hearings in this analysis is that 58 percent of the fire alarm hearings (twenty-two total) occurred in regard to regulatory policies. Considering the nature of regulations, the effect that failures to regulate a policy area effectively can have, and the high volume of lobbyists and interests tracking issues in regulatory policy domains, it is not surprising that Congress would find regulatory policy a place where many fire alarms would sound. For regulatory policy, there is the same pattern of witnesses as was noted earlier—agency witnesses predominate at fire alarm hearings, and trade association witnesses are less important. One other type of witness, the citizen group, declines in importance as well. Citizen groups testify, on average, half as often as trade associations, and in the case of fire alarms, testify at about half of all hearings. Considering the importance that many people attach to citizen groups as watchdogs over the activity of corporations (e.g., Berry 2000), it is surprising that they play such a small role in fire alarm hearings, especially during a period of Democratic control of the House.

Summary

Congressional committee activity is dominated by hearing activity. For any given program, committees typically hold at least one hearing evaluating some aspect of the program. Perhaps a dozen witnesses, representing federal agencies, trade groups, corporations, citizen groups, and other policy stakeholders, come before a committee to present testimony about why a program is or is not working as it should. Several scholars have argued that the expiration of a short-term authorization plays an important role in facilitating oversight, and interviews with congressional staff elicit similar views. However, the examination of hearings over a twenty-five-year period suggests that hearings occur throughout the life cycle of a program, regardless of its authorization status. Programs with expired authorizations continue to receive scrutiny, just as programs with active short-term authorizations are examined well before their authorization is about to expire. Committees have various incentives, including their desire to gain points in the media or with various interest groups, for holding hearings beyond a desire to consider specific policy changes.

6

Steering Agencies with Reauthorizations

Congress plays a key role in shaping federal agencies and the policies that they implement. Congress creates agencies through the legislative process, funds their operations through the appropriations process, structures the policies Congress will implement, and determines the actors with whom congressional members will work. As David Rosenbloom (2000) has noted, Congress reshaped itself after World War II in order to have better oversight and control over the administrative state. In less than two months in the summer of 1946, Congress passed the Legislative Reorganization Act (LRA) and the Administrative Procedures Act, with the explicit goal of better controlling federal agencies. "Agencies were reconceptualized as extensions of the legislature and, to some extent, its processes" (Rosenbloom 2000, 2).

Given that the goal of the LRA was to create greater watchfulness over agencies, there has often been a sharp focus on hearings in the study of oversight, and for good reason. Hearings are an important tool in a committee's repertory as they seek out information. Committee members want to have a clear understanding of the relationship between policies and their outcomes (Krehbiel 1991), and hearings are one mechanism they use to gather information. Additionally, hearings reap benefits for the committee's members beyond the collection of information; they are a focal point for the credit claiming, position taking, and advertising that members use to retain their jobs (Mayhew 1974). Furthermore, hearings allow members to receive recognition in their home states, often by bringing local witnesses to testify.

However, hearings are but one way that Congress is able to shape agency behavior. The reauthorization process is another key mechanism that Congress uses to oversee the federal bureaucracy and the vast networks that are involved in implementing public programs. By revisiting the status of a given program at set intervals, Congress is able to steer policy much in the same way that a captain steers a ship. Congress can gather information about a program between reauthorizations and then use this information to determine the direction and speed that the program should go for the next several years. If all is well, Congress may expand the scope of the program so that it can serve a larger client base. If the program is going to hit something—like the interest of an important group or the jurisdiction of another agency—Congress can move the program in another direction. Through reauthorizations, Congress plays a key role in forming the governance structures that shape the policy world (e.g., Lynn, Heinrich, and Hill 2001).

In the study of congressional oversight there is often a sharp focus on hearings, and for good reason. Hearings are an important tool in a committee's repertory as they seek out information. Committee members want to have a clear understanding of the relationship between policies and their outcomes (Krehbiel 1991), and hearings are one mechanism they use to gather information. Additionally, hearings reap benefits for the committee's members beyond the collection of information; they are a focal point for the credit claiming, position taking, and advertising that members use to retain their jobs (Mayhew 1974). Furthermore, hearings allow members to receive recognition in their home states, often by bringing local witnesses to testify.

In this chapter, I focus on how the renewal of a program's authorization facilitates a different type of control by Congress, the *ex ante* control that is exerted when laws are made or modified in a way that regulates the behavior of agencies and other policy players in a detailed, prescriptive manner. Ex ante control requires policy makers to be visionary as they seek to regulate actions in a way that promotes effective outcomes and avoids adverse consequences. This method of control also has implications for the implementation and management of the programs in question. The stability that arises from reauthorizing a given program only at fixed intervals is important for all actors in the process. All policy actors can know that procedures and rules can be put in place that will not be disrupted for a given period.

Three case studies are presented to illustrate how ex ante control works in a reauthorization environment. By examining Head Start, mass transit, and the Commodities Futures Trading Commission in detail, it is possible to see how Congress shapes these programs over time and changes their dynamics with each reauthorization. These changes often result in shifts in the structure of the program, how a program is implemented, and how the program is funded. By making these changes at fixed intervals, Congress is able to ensure that a program can continue to function optimally as the environment in which the program operates changes.

The Desire for Policy Control in Congress

When members of Congress create new programs, they typically want to control how the program is implemented. One way Congress achieves this goal is by hardwiring legislation in a way that institutes controls into the design of the agency and its regulatory scheme. This form of control is intended to help overcome the problem of bureaucratic drift by limiting the scope and discretion of agencies. However, while Congress does structure agencies through the legislative process, ex ante controls have generally been viewed as costly. Moe (1990, 228) provides a very nice articulation of the trade-offs encountered in this form of oversight. He notes that Congress can best control agencies by specifying

> in excruciating detail, precisely what the agency is to do and how it is to do it, leaving as little as possible to the discretionary judgment of bureaucrats—and thus as little as possible for future authorities to exercise control over, *short of passing new legislation*. [However,] this is not a formula for creating effective organizations. . . . [A]gencies are burdened with cumbersome, complicated, technically inappropriate structures that undermine their capacity to perform their jobs well (italics added).

The problem here is clear: the benefit to Congress of regulating agencies through the legislative process is undermined by the need to change structures and other agency resources as conditions change, and the only way to accomplish this is by more legislating (which is a costly activity). Of course, Congress can and does use short-term authorizations as an internal mechanism within legislation that facilitates the consideration and passage of future legislation. With this mechanism in place, Congress is better positioned to use the legislative process as a mechanism of control. The systematic use of legislation to control agencies is beneficial on several fronts. Perhaps most importantly, it provides Congress with the opportunity to do something with its knowledge on a specific issue. Given that members and committees have incentives to be informational experts on an issue, the renewal of a short-term authorization allows this information to be used in the legislative process. All of the hearings, the General Accounting Office reports, and other information that the committee gets from interest groups and the like can be channeled into legislative change in a reauthorization.

Designing Control Mechanisms

How does Congress use legislation to control an agency? Mathew McCubbins (1985) has identified several types of ex ante controls that

Congress can use to control agency behavior. First, Congress can limit the scope of an agency's activities, specifying the types of activities an agency can or cannot do as a part of implementing a program. For example, Congress can specify what types of targets are covered under an agency's regulatory umbrella, or what types of activities a program can fund. Second, Congress can limit the implementation tools that are at the disposal of an agency. For example, Congress may force an agency to directly provide a good or service to clients, or require that a given activity be contracted out. Third, Congress can establish the settings in which regulatory activities can occur. For example, Congress may limit agencies or their regulatory targets from using the courts to achieve their goals.

There are other sources of ex ante control, such as auditing procedures and reporting requirements, that can be built into legislation (Banks 1989; Banks and Weingast 1992; Bendor, Taylor, and Van Gallen 1985, 1987). This is a quite common form of control; an examination of laws that created new programs in the 89th and 103rd Congresses found that between 44 and 63 percent of these laws contained specific reporting requirements (Hall and O'Toole 2000). Congress can also specify the complexity of the relationships involved in the implementation of the program. For example, Congress may require multiple agencies, intergovernmental actors, and business or nonprofit actors to be involved in various aspects of the program implementation, and these complex implementation relationships are quite common (Hall and O'Toole 2000). Congress can also establish procedural requirements and preference aggregation methods that constrain the agency (e.g., McCubbins, Noll, and Weingast 1987).

The process of renewing a short-term authorization provides Congress with an opportunity to thoroughly reconsider the substantive legislation and examine the previously enacted ex ante controls, adjusting them so that the agency functions optimally. Agency discretion can be either constrained or loosened based on information from internal inputs—including auditing procedures, hearings, and reports from sources like the GAO and CBO—and from external inputs such as interest groups, the White House, and the agency itself. Congress can revise the control mechanisms that were incorporated into the original enactment based on information about the performance of the program when the authorization was active. The ability to modify these factors is important because, as McCubbins (1985, 725) notes: "Structural mechanisms seek to solve problems of agency shirking and slippage by constraining the substantive discretion of the administrative entity and by channeling the decision making within the administration to alternatives that are in compliance with congressional intent."

By examining how Congress changes these structural control mechanisms as they renew a program's authorizing legislation, it is possible to see the various ways in which an agency can be controlled or empowered, based on what Congress has learned through experience during the previous authorization and changes in the policy environment. The other analyses of short-term authorizations have focused on the use of multivariate analyses. Here, I examine ex ante changes more qualitatively by using case studies. For each of the three cases, I will focus on how institutional settings, regulatory scope, implementation instruments, procedural requirements, reporting requirements, and resource distributions changed over time.

Changing Head Start

In 1965, Project Head Start was created as an eight-week summer program run by the Office of Economic Opportunity. In the 1969 reauthorization of the program, Congress shifted the Head Start program to the Office of Child Development in the U.S. Department of Health, Education, and Welfare. Tracking the program across its reauthorizations since 1974, it is possible to see how the federal rules governing the program have changed over time. These changes have affected management both at the federal level and at local levels, where Head Start is implemented (often by local governments or not-for-profit organizations).

As table 6.1 shows, the 1974 authorization states the scope of the program, the services that must be provided, the targets to be served, and the formula to be used to distribute funds; it provides due process procedures for those entities who have grant applications that are rejected and for the evaluation of the program. In the 1981 reauthorization, the program formulas changed, the scope of the program was expanded, new targets were added, new standards were created for participation, and parental participation requirements in the management of local programs were expanded. The 1984 reauthorization required the Department of Education to provide training and technical assistance funding for Head Start and to provide that training and assistance in specific manners. Local Head Start providers were required to be physically located in the jurisdiction that they serve and HHS was to designate a Head Start agency in all communities that apply. The scope of the program was also expanded, and the department was banned from various actions that could result in programs being excluded or the number of participants or program services being reduced.

In each reauthorization during the 1990s (1990, 1994, and 1998) the Head Start program was changed, with Congress placing an increased emphasis on expanding the number of children served and on evaluating

Table 6.1 Ex Ante Control over Head Start through Reauthorizations

Year	Institutional Setting	Regulatory Scope	Instruments	Procedural Requirements	Reporting Required	Resource Distribution
1975	HEW; local providers	Criteria for agencies/children; service requirements	Grants/contracting rules; technical assistance	Appeals for rejected agencies; parental involvement		Formulas defined; technical assistance
1981	HHS; local providers	Services to Indians, migrants, disabled, children in poverty	New technical assistance	New fiscal, planning, and administrative standards; more parent involvement		Formula revised; new technical assistance
1984	HHS; local providers	Children can receive two years of service	Application rules; revised grant and funding u se rules; training	No performance standards changes; no block grants; agency must be in area served	Awards report	Formula and technical assistance revised
1986	HHS; locals					New formula
1990	HHS; locals	Specifies funding targets; expansion to unserved areas; regulate teacher quality	New program review tools; program evaluations; training	Facilitate locally developed service delivery models; new parent involve; notice/hearing rule for program change; teacher standards	Program status; service models; spec ial population services; longitudinal study	Formula requires maintenance of service levels
1994	HHS; locals; states; K–12 schools	New family service programs; collaborate w/ schools and other service providers; Indian reservations	H.S. fellowship program; mentor teacher program; training	Hours of daily service; model staff planning; teacher qualifications; training; expanded parental involvement	Worker benefits; need for all-day, all-year service; service needs of special population; longitudinal study	New formulas and allocation requirements
1998	HHS; locals; states; K–12 schools	New purpose: school readiness; new collaborations; service to new areas	New evaluation tools; new selection tools; new technical assistance	Teacher certification requirements; education performance standards; new designation rules	Program status; service models; program quality and impact	New formulas and allocation requirements

the effectiveness of local programs more thoroughly. The scope of these evaluations was specified in part by the law, but also required the development of standards for implementation. New staff qualifications were required, new definitions were created, new studies were required, new populations were to be served, and the scope of the program was changed to allow for all-day Head Start programs. By the end of the decade, the priority in Head Start switched from expanding the program to improving the quality of Head Start programs. These legislative changes required federal managers to modify the type and scope of service they provided.

At its heart, Head Start is a multifaceted contracting program; there are more than 1,460 grantees that provide services to more than 782,000 children in 711,000 families (GAO/HEHS-98–65). When the program first was being implemented, it was primarily focused on providing grants to local service providers. However, Congress has mandated that federal managers also develop standards for the program, evaluate the program, provide technical support for the program, provide curricular support to grantees, and support coordination between Head Start and other federal programs. They must also evaluate the credentials of grantees (federal law requires that grantees be located within the area where they provide services), ensure that funds are being allocated appropriately—Head Start has a very complex funding formula—and audit to make sure that these funds are being spent on appropriate activities. These responsibilities have evolved over time; currently, the curricular and evaluation aspects of the program are being most strongly promoted, largely because of congressional pressure (GAO-HEHS-09–183).

The changes that have come to Head Start during reauthorizations have also required local managers to provide services to new populations in different ways and at increasing levels of quality. Under Head Start rules, local managers are required to provide a 25 percent match for the federal funding received. In addition to this fund-raising requirement, however, Head Start has also required local managers to manage expanding parental involvement requirements, with planning and advisory groups having a say in how local programs are governed. They have had to develop new service delivery models, document how effectively they work, and hire a better quality staff according to new rules that strictly govern who can serve as a Head Start instructor. More importantly, however, the entire way in which the program is framed at the local level has changed, with the focus now being centered more and more on the educational services that students receive, with somewhat less emphasis given to the overall services—including health and social-welfare services—that these children need.

Changing Transit Policy

Like Head Start, the federal mass transit program is a product of the Johnson administration. With the passage of the Urban Mass Transportation Act of 1964, Congress began the process of providing funding for local mass transit. Also like Head Start, the mass transit program was moved during an early reauthorization; in 1968, the agency was moved from the Department of Housing and Urban Development to the newly created Department of Transportation. An examination of the last four transit reauthorizations illustrates the legislative dynamic for a highly distributive program.

The transit reauthorization process was added to the broader surface transportation authorization process, which historically focused on highways, when the 1978 transit reauthorization was incorporated into the broader surface transportation bill. Title III of the 1978 surface transportation legislation was the Federal Public Transportation Act (FPTA), and almost the entire section focused on how transit money could and could not be spent. The FPTA contained overall spending levels for various transit programs and authorized specific transit new starts, so that certain cities could begin building rail projects. It revised the formulas for the distribution of transit grant funds and specified who has control over spending the money. The FPTA set matching rates for transit programs, specifying how much money states and localities must spend to match federal contributions. It also set up grant programs for special populations such as the elderly, people with disabilities, and rural communities. Table 6.2 details the programs' reauthorization histories.

The 1982 transit reauthorization looked much like the 1978 law. It contained the same types of spending levels for programs, specified new starts, tweaked the funding formulas, and specified who could and could not spend transit money and the way in which the money could be spent. However, the 1982 act also included something new, a Mass Transit Account in the Highway Trust Fund. The Highway Trust Fund is the account into which all gas tax revenues have historically been deposited. These tax revenues accrue in the account and are, according to members of the authorizing committees, supposed to be spent on highways. Of course, appropriators have a different view; they believe in unified budgeting in which trust fund accounts are all part of the same big pool of resources. There have long been battles between authorizers and appropriators regarding whether surface transportation spending should equal the amount of revenues in the Highway Trust Fund. By putting two cents of the gas tax into a separate transit account, authorizers were allowing

Table 6.2 Ex Ante Control over Mass Transit through Reauthorizations

	Institutional Setting	Regulatory Scope	Instruments	Procedural Requirements	Reporting Required	Resource Distribution to Targets
1978	Secretary of Transportation	•Stipulates who receives funds			•Report on status of all programs •Study on alternate funding formulas •Study low-cost bus services	•Revised apportionment formulas •Sets federal-local match rates •Formula grants to low-population areas
1982		•Limits who can receive grants •Repeals safety program requirements	•Secretary must notify Congress about future obligations		•Biennial report on transit needs •Study of alternate funding mechanisms	•Lists specific special projects
1987		•Expands activities available for grants	•Requires long-term planning	•Requires secretary to list all proposed rule-making activity in federal register	•Report on all transit needs	•Increased cost sharing for states that enhance accessibility of systems •Grants for safety •Lists special projects
1991	Creates Metropolitan Planning Organizations to allocate funds in urban areas	•Requires urban areas to have congestion management plan	•Streamlines local reporting to secretary •Allows secretary to withhold funds if safety improvements are not made		•Report on transit safety •Report on how transit funds are spent at state and local levels	•Increases federal match rates •Adjusts allocation formulas •Lists special projects •Allows reallocation of highway funds to transit

transit interests to make a specific claim on a specific amount of revenues for their programs.

The 1987 reauthorization was not much different from the previous two, but the 1991 bill was a watershed, much like the 1982 legislation. The catalyst for the changes in 1991 was a different reauthorization from the previous year, the passage of amendments to the Clean Air Act. A coalition of environmental groups played a key role in the passage of the Clean Air Act amendments, and these stakeholders used their newfound clout and access to influence transportation policy. Because the cleanliness of the air is directly affected by transportation, these groups saw the 1991 authorization as yet another opportunity to strengthen environmental policy. As a general rule, the environmental coalition does not like highways but thinks highly of mass transit, so they worked to make the 1991 Intermodal Surface Transportation Efficiency Act (ISTEA) into a transit bill. Granted, most of the money in the bill continued to be spent on highways; however, these groups also made highway funds highly fungible for use in transit projects, while making transit funds completely nonfungible. For example, metropolitan areas that violated clean air standards could no longer use federal highway funds to build new roads, but they could use these funds for transit. The bill also authorized more new starts, expanded transit funding, and granted greater transit access to disadvantaged individuals.

Changing the Commodity Futures Trading Commission

Both the Head Start and mass transit programs are distributive or redistributive in nature. As we turn to examining the Commodity Futures Trading Commission (CFTC), we can see the differences between regulatory and distributive programs. The CFTC was created in 1974 with the passage of H.R. 13113, moving commodity regulation from the U.S. Department of Agriculture into the new agency. As would be expected, the 1974 law structures the new agency—creating a commission—and outlines its regulatory reach. It states what types of commodities are under the jurisdiction of the CFTC, what types of activities are unlawful under the act, and what penalties can be imposed under the law. As McCubbins (1985) notes, Congress is quite interested in ensuring that regulatory policy is implemented in a specific way, and by limiting the regulatory tools available to an agency and the number and type of stakeholders covered by regulations, Congress can ensure that the agency is limited in its authority.

The three reauthorizations that followed the 1974 inaugural bill illustrate how the expiration of short-term authorizations created for Congress an opportunity to adjust the regulatory mechanisms an agency has at its disposal and the number of stakeholders covered by the agency's jurisdiction. In 1978, the law was modified in several fundamental ways. First, the agency's structure was changed so that a chairman appointed by the president would govern the CFTC. Second, certain types of commodity traders were excluded from the jurisdiction of the commission. Third, the scope of the financial penalties that could be levied by the commission was expanded, as were its powers to hold hearings and grant immunity to witnesses. Finally, the U.S. district courts were made the court of jurisdiction for the commission's work. Table 6.3 details the reauthorization history of the Commodities Futures Trading Commission.

In 1982, the primary focus of the reauthorization was to delimit the jurisdictions of the CFTC and the Securities and Exchange Commission and to expand the rulemaking powers of the CFTC. Specifically, Congress granted the CFTC the authority over foreign futures trading in the United States, allowed it to limit speculative futures, and broadened the scope of activities under the CFTC's jurisdiction. It also ensured that the SEC retained its historical jurisdiction over securities by barring the CFTC from regulating securities indices. The bill also allowed the CFTC to charge fees for certain services, a provision that would help the CFTC fund certain activities. In the *Congressional Quarterly Almanac* summary of the 1982 legislation, the listing of provisions almost all focus on how the

Table **6.3** Ex Ante Control over CFTC through Reauthorizations

	Institutional Setting	Regulatory Scope	Instruments	Procedural Requirements	Reporting Required	Resource Distribution to Targets
1974	Commission	Targets identified	Fines set; reparations to victims; Trade Association created	Rule promulgation	Reports required	
1978	Federal District Court jurisdiction	Excludes cash dealers	Subpoena witness; increased fines	On-record hearings; enhanced APA Requirements	Reports to FED, SEC, Treasury required	
1982	Judicial Review in Courts of Appeal	Excludes foreign currency; covers foreign futures, precious metals	Requires Trade Associations to enforce CFTC rules; allows registration disqualifications	New rules on when ALJ must hear case	Study of futures trading on economy	
1986		Excludes foreign boards of trade	Subpoena foreign witness; Trade Association discipline requirements		GAO study of cattle futures	
1991	CFTC can seek monetary damage in Civil Court		Increased fines; customer restitution; makes certain violations felonies	Must publish dissenting opinions	Compliance report; computerized future trading report	
1995	One sentence reauthorizing entire program					

authorization shapes the scope of the agency's jurisdiction, the tools it can apply as a regulator, and the venues for implementing its regulatory powers. The law also required that several studies be conducted by the CFTC.

By 1992, when Congress finally reauthorized the CFTC, the authorization legislation was more technical in nature. The major issue in the authorization was how to handle new financial instruments known as swaps, hybrids, and derivatives. The decision of Congress was to exempt these new financial instruments from regulation until two studies were completed in 1994; Congress scheduled the CFTC authorization to expire in 1995 so that it could take advantage of this information. The law also made a series of technical changes to the regulatory powers of the CFTC, allowing them, for example, to conduct undercover sting operations.

Facilitating Implementation

As these cases show, major changes can and do occur as Congress reshapes programs during the reauthorization process. These changes fit nicely into Bardach's (1977) conception of implementation as a game in which different sets of stakeholders in the process attempt to achieve their goals by manipulating the system in specific ways. Each player deploys a different strategy as she tries to achieve specific goals, such as getting larger budgets, getting pork barrel projects, obstructing the implementation until the program dies, gaining turf, or building their personal reputation. These games often get in the way of efficient and effective implementation because different policy players are attempting to achieve their own goals without attempting to achieve the goal intended by the crafters of the legislation.

Legislators do not want the policies that they have crafted to be subverted by other policy players. Bardach (1977, 273–78) recognizes this and argues that there is a critical role to be played by "fixers," who are often the legislators involved in crafting the legislation that is being implemented. Much like the crooked boxing promoter, the implementation fixer is trying to game the system so that she can get the outcome she wants. She fixes the game by changing the rules, often by changing aspects of the law that allow policy players to play games.

If the implementation process is a game, then short-term authorizations can be viewed as an effort to regularize opportunities for these fixers to change the rules of the game to get an outcome that is preferable to them. Consider the case of the CFTC. The CFTC reauthorizations allowed legislators to make small but critical changes in the law governing futures trading. In most cases the types of regulatory mechanisms made available to the agency were expanded so that the CFTC could work more effectively. As each authorization expired, past fixes could be evaluated and new changes made so that the implementation of commodity futures trading regulations was operating as the Congress and president desired.

In addition to fixing the rules of the game, authorization legislation determines how long the game will remain fixed. Defense policy remains fixed for only one year, whereas many domestic policies remain fixed for five or six years. For many policy players, having the game fixed for five or six years is crucial because it can take that long just to initiate the implementation process. The Economic Development Agency's work in Oakland, which Pressman and Wildavsky (1984) studied, took more than four years just to get off the ground. Other programs, such as education programs, often take several years to become operational as well. Once these programs start functioning, they also benefit from longer authorizations because the policy players can then play for the future knowing that the rules of engagement will remain the same for some period.

Fixing the game is also critical for the states and localities who often have to implement these programs. Authorizations provide states with some certainty about the funding levels they will be receiving, which allows them to plan for the future. One former state transportation official stated:

> You can't just turn a battle ship or our transportation program on a dime. Many states have a five-year work plan so—here is the perfect example— ISTEA passes in 1991. Each year we have to figure out how to plan for the

next year. Two years into ISTEA, we have to figure out what the first post-ISTEA year will be like. The longer the bill the better from a policy perspective and planning perspective because we have to match up the money with the programs and plans.

For implementers and policy makers alike, the reauthorization process allows for key parts of the implementation process to be tweaked. Formal networks can be adjusted. Goals can be made clearer. Policy inconsistencies can be addressed. Resources can be requested. The authority of implementers can be adjusted. The incentives for various implementers can be adjusted to encourage cooperation. Each of these components of the implementation process can be the key to a successful policy outcome (Edwards and Sharkansky 1978; Nakamura and Smallwood 1980). For example, programs that are started as small pilots are often expanded at the next reauthorization. An education lobbyist noted:

The 21st Century Schools program was a small federal grant program that was run by the department here in Washington. After five years, teachers, the Department, and the states all realized that the program would work better if the grant program was administered by the states. You need time to figure out how to implement a program like this, and a five year authorization gives you that time, and the opportunity to make the change.

Policy makers—especially members of the committee with jurisdiction over the policy in question—have strong incentives to make sure that the programs under their jurisdiction are implemented effectively and operate as promised, and that the expiration of an authorization is the time when these changes can be made. One of the benefits that accrue to programs with four- or five-year authorizations is that there is time to assess the effectiveness of the program. As one education policy player observed, "[W]e are talking real dollars here and they require real assessment. Over four or five years, you can give a program the evaluation it deserves. You can ensure that the process of getting the money out the door is effective, and that the program produces a quality outcome." A person who has served as a congressional staffer reiterated this point: "With election years every two years, you can imagine that House members would want to do this bill more, but if we had authorizations that were shorter than five years, the states and locals would go batty and we would make a lot of bad policy."

Summary

Even though the Head Start, transit, and CFTC reauthorizations resulted in legislation that is quite different, the purpose and outcomes are quite similar. In each case, parties affected by the legislation battled to achieve an outcome that was most beneficial to them. The transit reauthorization is primarily a battle about who gets what. Because of the limited pool of funds that exists for any particular program, these fights are very contentious, as funding for one state or one city inevitably means that another state or city does not get the funding it wants. The same is true for the regulation of commodities, although in this case, the battle is not over who gets what, but rather who gets regulated and how. Each CFTC reauthorization shapes the way in which commodity trading can be regulated, the types of penalties that can be used to punish those who violate the rules, and the procedures for due process that are available to the punished. The Head Start case illustrates how Congress changes the law governing a program with the intent of shaping how the program is implemented and managed. With each reauthorization, interest groups are able to make claims about how the law should be changed based on experience gained during the previous authorization period. These groups conduct a variety of activities—such as commissioning studies of how the law has been implemented, testifying at hearings, lobbying, and similar behaviors—to explain why the law should be changed to fix implementation problems.

7

Policy Control and
Short-Term Authorizations

"Getting something done between authorizations is a bitch."
—Former transportation lobbyist

If short-term authorizations are an important mechanism for agenda and policy control for authorizing committees, then their use should drive when legislative changes do and do not occur. The conceptualization outlined in chapter 3 stated that this mechanism would place a particular policy on the legislative agenda at a specific time for possible modification, legislation would be passed, and then the policy would not be modified again until the next reauthorization. This process ensures that the status quo remains in effect and the policy has an opportunity to be implemented by various stakeholders. By having policies come onto and off of their agenda at specific times, committees are able to wield power within the chamber, affect a given policy domain on a regular basis, and ensure that policy in a given domain can remain stable long enough for success or failure to be established. In this chapter, I test whether changes in an authorization's status, media coverage, and hearings influence legislative activity in a given policy area. I specifically consider whether short-term authorizations influence the timing of passage of legislative enactments in Congress, and affect the way in which committees address policy issues.

Short-Term Authorizations and Policy Change

Short-term authorizations regularize the policy process, allowing change to occur at the time scheduled in the program's authorization. An individual who works for the U.S. Department of Education noted that if the legislation undergirding education policy were permanent, it would make the policy process very difficult. "If there were not these reauthorizations, if the programs were permanent, then there would be these disjointed changes to programs that would not fit together into a coherent policy. Otherwise, you would have to pick and pull it apart in order to change anything."[1] Short-term authorizations allow for change to be made coherently at regularized intervals, giving policy players the opportunity to educate members and to shape or reshape a policy's definition before the issue is addressed in the legislative arena.

Scholars interested in policy change are correct to examine hearings and media coverage as being important to policy change. However, an important question is whether these factors lead to meaningful policy change, which typically manifests itself through changes to the underlying legislation. In fact, it is not clear that changes in policy equilibria occurring outside of the reauthorization process lead to changes in the law when there is an existing short-term authorization that is scheduled to expire at some point in the relatively near future. Obviously, hearings do result in learning and can result in changes in a policy's definition. However, it is not clear that any legislative actions can be taken outside the authorization cycle. In interviews, individuals involved in the federal policy process suggested that reauthorization legislation is typically seen as the primary vehicle for facilitating policy change. One agency staffer noted that "everything needs a vehicle, and the reauthorization bills are the biggest around."[2] Reauthorization bills are especially important for members of the minority party in the House. One minority party staffer who handles education policy noted, "[F]or people in the minority, life is driven by reauthorizations because they are the main vehicles that will come out of committee."

The type of policies that the media and many scholars focus on in their studies may in part influence the lack of focus on the importance of authorizations. Much work has been done with a focus on cases, such as health care reform, where many groups are mobilized in a highly public way in the legislative process. In the case of the 1992–94 health care debate, the argument was over how to create something new. However, as Schick (1983) noted, the normal world of legislative activity is dominated by short-term authorizations.

Analyzing Policy Change with Short-Term Authorizations

This examination considers whether a specific kind of policy control mechanism—the expiration of a short-term authorization—leads to legislative activity that results in lawmaking by Congress and the president. This last point is critical. As noted previously, there are many things that lead Congress to hold hearings, and scholars such as Baumgartner and Jones

(1993) have aptly noted that hearings can play a critical role in shaping the way in which a given policy is viewed by Congress and the public at large. However, I hypothesize that policy change that fundamentally alters a policy domain generally requires legislative enactment, and Congress does not change policy in many policy domains and for many key programs until the expiration of a short-term authorization. That is, hearings, media coverage, and other factors may influence the policy change process on a broad level and the breadth of the change that occurs, but short-term authorizations are the trigger, the point at which Congress actually allows the legislative change for a given policy to occur. I test three research questions to determine which factors most strongly influence legislative activity.

- Does increased hearing activity on a specific policy issue lead to the passage of legislation by Congress to address this issue?
- Does increased media coverage of a specific policy issue lead to the passage of legislation by Congress to address this issue?
- Does the expiration of a short-term authorization lead to the passage of legislation to reauthorize the program and to make changes in this specific policy area?

The first two hypotheses address specific concerns of the ACF and punctuated equilibrium theories of policy change. Media coverage and hearings are two points where information comes to the fore that shapes the image of a policy and fundamental knowledge of a policy. If these factors lead to policy change directly, then their presence, and changes in their levels, should trigger legislative action. If short-term authorizations are critical to determining the timing and success of legislative change, then it should be the dominant variable in the model. In this case, short-term authorizations would serve as a mechanism for committees to control their environment. Legislation would pass when an authorization expires, as the committee funnels policy activity for a given program into a specific fixed point in time, helping to augment gatekeeping by keeping the agenda free for other activities.

The hearing and legislative enactment data used in this analysis come primarily from the Agendas Project at the University of Washington. These data were combined with data on authorization status from USCCAN and media data from the annual *Readers' Guide to Periodical Literature*. The hypotheses noted previously are again tested in four policy areas: education, transportation, regulatory, and Social Security, with the specific programs used in the analysis listed in table 5.1.

The data for each time series were analyzed in three ways. First, the data were entered and pooled to allow for a pooled cross-sectional time series analysis across all programs. Second, the data were analyzed by policy area using cross-sectional time series analysis, with data for each program entered by year, and then pooled with data for other similar programs. Third, the data were analyzed by program instead of by policy, and, instead of using a dichotomous dependent variable, I use the number of bills passed in each year. More information about how the data were pooled can be found in the Methodological Appendix.

Several independent variables are tested in this analysis. The primary independent variable is whether it is an authorization year (authorization year = 1). The other two primary dependent variables are the number of hearings held and the number of media stories on the topic each year.[3] Two control variables are included in the model to ensure that change in party control of different branches does not independently influence the findings, whether Democrats (coded 1) controlled Congress and whether the Democrats controlled the presidency (coded 1). One variable that is not included in the analysis shown in this chapter and the next is a variable that contains hearings lagged by one year. This variable was tested but does not produce results markedly different from those produced with the hearing variable not lagged. In order to make the results more parsimonious, it is not included in the tables that follow.

I begin this analysis by examining how the five factors noted earlier—hearings, the expiration of an authorization, media coverage, partisan control of Congress, and divided government—correlate with the actual enactment of legislation in each issue area. Table 7.1 summarizes these correlations. The data show two factors with the passage of laws in a given program area in a given year across all program areas. The first factor is the expiration of a program's authorization, and the second factor is the amount of media coverage in that year. For all programs with short-term authorizations, the expiration of a short-term authorization strongly correlates with the enactment of legislation, with media coverage also correlating, but at a weaker level. Public hearings do correlate with the enactment of legislation in the overall model, but this is likely the result of the importance of hearings in one policy area, transportation. For other policy areas, hearings do not significantly correlate with the enactment of legislation. Although not included in table 7.1, the number of hearings held in the preceding year also does not significantly correlate with the enactment of legislation. In addition, for the one permanently authorized program (Social Security) there are no significant variables that correlate with legislative activity.

The correlations present a preliminary indication of the role that short-term authorizations play in facilitating legislative change. A more comprehensive test of the hypotheses regarding policy change can be examined through the use of a fixed effects logit model, controlling for both the cross-sectional

Table 7.1 Factors That Correlate with Legislative Enactments, 1970–1994

	All Programs	Education	Transportation	Regulatory	Social Security
Authorization Year	0.56** (0.00)	0.77** (0.00)	0.56** (0.00)	0.52** (0.00)	—
Hearings Held	0.18** (0.00)	0.06 (0.59)	0.26** (0.01)	0.12 (0.23)	0.09 (0.68)
Media Coverage	0.26** (0.00)	0.45** (0.00)	0.17** (0.09)	0.41** (0.00)	0.02 (0.91)
Divided Congress	0.07 (0.25)	-0.09 (0.37)	0.22** (0.03)	0.09 (0.40)	-0.03 (0.88)
Divided Government	0.04 (0.51)	-0.06 (0.57)	0.06 (0.54)	0.10 (0.31)	0.03 (0.88)

Note: Dashes indicate that the variable is not included in a specific model.
**Correlation is significant at the 0.05 level (2 -tailed).

and the time series nature of the data. The enactment of legislation is the dependent variable, and the five factors noted above are the independent variables. Table 7.2 shows the results of this analysis for the full model, with each independent variable in a row, followed by the estimated model coefficient, the odds ratio for that variable, and the significance level. As expected, the model shows that the expiration of an authorization is critical to moving the legislative process in Congress and the decision to enact legislation.

The expected impact of the expiration of authorizations on the passage of a new law in a policy area when all other variables are held at their means is also significant. The far right column in table 7.2 presents the likely expected change in the dependent variable when the independent variable moves in either direction one standard deviation, in the case of continuous variables, or from zero to one in the case of dummy variables. For example, moving from an off year to an authorization year increases the likelihood of a law being passed by almost 50 percent. This is not to say that the other variables do not have an impact, but the changes that are expected from even dramatic shifts in their levels are much smaller. For example, if media coverage moves from one standard deviation below the mean to one standard deviation above the mean, the likelihood of legislation passing increases by only 7 percent.[4]

These findings illustrate the benefit of a short-term authorization: it shields a given policy from having policy change occur based on perturbations in the political or policy environment. Instead, the expiration of an authorization structures the timing of legislative changes to public policy. One former congressional staffer noted, "For something to happen between

Table 7.2 Logistic Regression: Factors Influencing the Passage of
          Legislation, Full Model

Variables	Coefficient	Odds Ratio	Significance	Expected Change, Dep. Var.
Authorization Year	3.61	37.13	0.00	0.48
Hearings	0.06	1.06	0.12	0.11
Media Coverage	0.021	1.02	0.07	0.07
Divided Congress	0.72	2.06	0.07	-0.05
Divided Government	-0.30	0.74	0.46	0.12

$N = 300$
Log likelihood $= -123.65$
LR chi^2 $= 140.14$
Prob. >chi^2= 0.00

authorizations would require a consensus among members and the initiative of a well-placed member. You aren't going to roll the chairman on something that is out of order like that." Short-term authorizations provide order to a process that could otherwise become chaotic. An education policy staffer noted that when change does occur between authorizations, it is "typically the result of the agency not doing their job correctly." In essence, changes between authorizations are often an effort to conduct oversight via legislative activity.

Short-Term Authorizations in Education Policy

Before looking at the findings of multivariate analyses examining the impact of the use of short-term authorizations in education policy, it is beneficial to study the evolution of lawmaking in a policy area, starting at its inception, before there was a short-term authorization process, through the passage of specific legislation to address the policy in question. Consider, for example, education programs for people with disabilities. This case is an illustrative example of the power of two features of the modern legislative process: consolidated programs and short-term authorizations. Before the passage of the Education of All Handicapped Children Act 1975, programs for people with disabilities were handled on an ad hoc basis. Congress would pass a program here for the education of people who are blind, a program there for the education of people with mental retardation, and another program for the education of people with hearing impairments. These programs were permanent when created, and they contained no authorization of appropriations language. Laws were passed whenever it seemed appropriate.

Since the passage of the 1975 act, Congress has treated disability education in a structured manner. Congress began passing disabilities laws in years when the authorization of a program expired. Since the consolidated act was passed, Congress has considered programs for the education of people with disabilities in a comprehensive fashion and has enacted legislation at the scheduled time—when the authorization is set to expire. The close relationship between the expiration of an authorization and the passage of a new law can be contrasted to the more random relationship between public laws passed and hearings being held. Oversight hearings examining the issue of education for people with disabilities have been held throughout the life cycle of this program, with several hearings often being held in Congress, but there is less of a direct relationship between hearing activity and legislative activity. Of course, what goes on at these hearings can have a direct impact on how subsequent legislation is shaped, but the hearings themselves do not seem to move Congress to enact legislation unless the authorization of a program is about to expire.

A multivariate analysis of four education programs—vocational education, Head Start, disabilities education, and funding for the National Endowment for the Arts, which has a broader educational purpose than the other three—illustrates how short-term authorizations work to structure and control change in education policy. As was the case previously, the data for education policy strongly support the contention that short-term authorizations are an important mechanism for controlling policy change, as defined by changes in the law. The odds ratio for the expiration of an authorization variable shows how important the expirations of authorizations are for determining whether legislation will be passed in a given year (table 7.3). By contrast, the remaining variables have odds ratios near one, suggesting that they are less important factors in determining when legislative activity will occur.

Additionally, I again tested to determine whether the expected impact of each independent variable on the likely passage of a new law in a policy area when all other variables are held at their means is also significant. The far right column in table 7.3 shows that in education policy, moving from an off year to an authorization year increases the likelihood of a law being passed by 52 percent in an authorization year. Increased media coverage— coverage that is one standard deviation above the mean—increases the likelihood of a law being passed by only 11 percent, and the hearings variable changes by only 8 percent.[5]

Table 7.3 Logistic Regression: Factors Influencing the Passage of
Legislation, Education Model

Variables	Coefficient	Odds Ratio	Significance	Expected Change, Dep. Var.
Authorization Year	4.15	63.52	0.00	0.52
Hearings	0.16	1.17	0.32	0.08
Media Coverage	1.29	3.64	0.08	0.11
Divided Congress	-0.24	0.79	0.79	-0.12
Divided Government	-0.86	0.42	0.37	-0.06

$N = 100$
Log likelihood $= -23.67$
LR chi^2 = 64.94
Prob. chi^2 = 0.00

Not surprisingly, because short-term authorizations serve to greatly limit the likelihood of legislative activity, this also impacts other aspects of member behavior. A recent study (Harbridge 2003) found that bill introductions for several education programs correlate strongly with the expiration of the program's authorization. For Head Start, higher education, and the Elementary and Secondary Education Act, the expiration of an authorization leads to a concomitant increase in the number of bill introductions. Members clearly recognize that for programs with short-term authorizations, the action occurs when the authorization ends.

These findings are also confirmed by interviews with staffers who have worked in education policy. Consider how one agency person described her work:

When we came off of the ESEA [Elementary and Secondary Education Act] reauthorization, we went straight into preparing for the budget. Then, on the policy side, we have the special ed reauthorization, and we are starting to prepare for the higher ed and [vocational education] reauthorizations.[6]

Policy stakeholders often describe their lives as a series of reauthorizations. A person who has worked as a congressional staffer on education policy noted that the debate over reauthorizing the Head Start program does not even begin until the year the authorization expires, because several other programs for children expire the year before the Head Start bill does: "Everyone may be talking about Head Start before it expires, but the fact of the matter is, nothing was going to be done about it until it expires."[7]

The typical authorization for an education policy is for five years, which many see as being optimal for this policy area. As one person noted, in education policy "reauthorizations allow Congress and the administration to change the law with some frequency. . . . But the authorizations need to run long enough to take the idea, attach money to it, get the money out the door and implemented, and then evaluate the program's performance. Then you can say, 'this is good.'"[8] As this Department of Education executive notes, using short-term authorizations as a control mechanism also serves to benefit public managers who must implement programs. By creating a stable policy environment, managers are able to get a program rolling and collect data on how effective their efforts have been before they have to consider changes in the law again.

Authorizing Transportation Policy

The second policy area that I examine is transportation policy. The programs considered here are Amtrak, the Coast Guard, the Federal Aviation Administration, and urban mass transit. These programs cross all aspects of transportation policy—air, sea, and land—and programs with both distributive and regulatory purposes. Table 7.4 shows the findings of the multivariate analysis, which is methodologically identical to the analyses done for education programs. The expiration of authorization is again the dominant factor that affects the likelihood that a law will pass. The other variables in the model are not only insignificant; they also have a slight negative impact on the likelihood that a given law will pass. The far right column in table 7.4 shows that moving from an off year to an authorization year increases the likelihood that a transportation law will be passed by 70 percent.[9]

Other data support the contention of a strong a linkage between bill introductions and the expiration of an authorization. Harbridge (2003) found that there was a strong correlation between the number of highway bills introduced into Congress and the expiration of surface transportation legislation. She found that the number of transportation bills doubles or triples in a year when the program's authorization expires, from an average of approximately nineteen bill introductions in an off year to more than seventy—for example, in 1991, when the surface transportation legislation expired.

Transportation policy players note that the fights over the allocation of money that occur in the transportation bills are so intense that the com-

Table 7.4 Logistic Regression: Factors Influencing the Passage of
Legislation, Transportation Model

Variables	Coefficient	Odds Ratio	Significance	Expected Change, Dep. Var.
Authorization Year	3.96	52.22	0.00	0.7049
Hearings	-0.12	0.89	0.36	-0.0210
Media Coverage	-0.01	1.00	0.62	-0.2035
Divided Congress	2.20	9.04	0.01	0.4972
Divided Government	-0.40	0.67	0.61	-0.0753

$N = 100$
Log likelihood = -29.12
LR chi^2 = 42.79
Prob. > chi^2 = 0.00

mittee with jurisdiction—the Public Works Committee until 1994, now the Transportation and Infrastructure Committee—will not even consider bringing up these bills between authorizations. One person who has worked on numerous surface transportation authorizations said:

> You almost have to have authorization bills every so often to provide new directions for every program, and it serves to justify the committee . . . but it is such a huge and monumental task to strike the bargains and craft the deals to make one of these work, that it has to end with a long authorization. If you didn't [make the authorization long], it would dominate congress and committee agendas too much. You would have donor state fights, and you would have pork barrel fights that would be too great to handle.[10]

The battles over projects and the allocation of funding to the states leave the committees fighting until the last moment to get a bill passed. A former transportation committee staffer noted:

> The committee does not move between authorizations because there is no "have to" without a funding expiration or something similar. Even with a trigger [to end the flow of funds to states if an authorization is not completed], funding to states have [sic] lapsed in the last two authorizations. People just can't bear to go through the process more than once every six years. Hell, we can't even get technical corrections bills passed. The 1991 bill was written in the middle of the night and riddled with errors, but

there was no way to fix it. We finally fixed it when we did the NHS [legis-
lation creating the National Highway System], and it only passed because
of the money trigger that it had.[11]

Because transportation has such a large lobby of support among rank-
and-file members—all of whom want a project in the bill—and because the
bill is so large, congressional leaders dislike bringing up this legislation.
Few people realize that transportation is the largest nonmilitary domestic
discretionary program, and with the budget issues associated with its trust
funds, it is a policy issue many would like to avoid.

Authorizing Regulatory Policy

The final policy area examined in this analysis is regulatory policy, which
includes four programs—the Commodity Futures Trading Commission,
the Consumer Product Safety Commission, the Nuclear Regulatory
Commission, and the Securities and Exchange Commission. The results of
the multivariate analyses provide results similar to those found for education and transportation policy, although the other variables also produce
substantively significant results. Table 7.5 shows that the expiration of an
authorization variable is the dominant and most significant variable in the
model. The impact of the expiration of an authorization greatly increases
the odds that a law will be passed. Also, looking at the expected change in
the likelihood of a law being passed, the values for expected change are
smaller than in the earlier models.[12]

People who work in regulatory policy note that there are several reasons
why reauthorizations dominate the legislative landscape. In regulatory policy, one reason this is the case is that there is often a high level of conflict on
the issue. One person who has worked for a regulatory agency stated:

> I see reauthorizations as being like the business cycle. You rest, regroup,
> and come back to engage in some WWI trench warfare. It is not all war-
> fare, some of it is cooperative and we try to create alliances with groups
> whenever we can. But most of the time, there is industry on one side and
> us and the consumer groups on the other, battling it out.[13]

However, one key difference between regulatory policy and transportation policy is that regulatory issues are often very difficult to understand.
The difficulty of the issues can give Congress an incentive to consider them
collectively, when members have the time to focus on them and decrease
their learning curve. A former congressional staffer noted that "you have to

Table 7.5 Logistic Regression: Factors Influencing the Passage of
Legislation, Regulatory Model

Variables	Coefficient	Odds Ratio	Significance	Expected Change, Dep. Var.
Authorization Year	2.58	13.15	0.00	0.1739
Hearings	-0.02	1.00	0.82	-0.0133
Media Coverage	0.07	1.06	0.07	0.0772
Divided Congress	0.19	1.21	0.75	0.0132
Divided Government	0.156	1.17	0.81	0.0120

$N = 100$
Log likelihood = -41.45
LR chi^2 = 28.86
Prob. > chi^2 = 0.00
Pseudo R^2 = 0.22

remember, members are not going to spend all of their waking hours on
[that issue], or any issue, especially if it is difficult to understand." Although
some reauthorizations are big deals and some simply extend the program,
little action occurs in-between the expiration of the authorization.

Examining Short-Term Authorizations by Program

The final analysis I use is a Poisson regression to examine the impact of
short-term authorizations—that is, how short-term authorizations affect
policy. In this model, I estimate the maximum likelihood of the number of
occurrences, expressed as counts, of an event, which in this case is the likelihood that a law will pass. This analysis also uses a slightly different dependent variable, which is the number of bills passed in each year. This
dependent variable is highly bounded; its value never exceeds five, and in
9 percent of the cases the value is zero, one, or two. The findings of this
analysis are presented in table 7.6. For each program in the model, the
authorization variable remains a powerful determinant of legislative activity for each program; it is the variable that drives the model. The media and
hearings variables have little substantive significance in this program-by-
program analysis. Even in cases where there is a larger amount of legislative activity in a specific program area, the factors typically associated with
policy change do not seem to be driving the legislative process.

Table 7.6 The Impact of Short-Term Authorizations on
         Policy Change, by Program

	Coefficient	Standard Error	Z	$P > \lvert z \rvert$
Authorization Year	1.43	0.17	8.10	0.00
Number of Hearings	0.06	0.03	-0.70	0.49
Amount of Media Coverage	0.02	0.01	-0.69	0.49
Divided Congress	-0.30	0.17	1.21	0.23
Divided Government	0.72	0.19	-0.61	0.55

$N = 300$
Wald chi^2(4) = 77.43
Prob. > chi^2 = 0.00
Log likelihood = -123.65

The Social Security Control Case

If variables such as media coverage and hearings held were important factors influencing the passage of legislation in Congress, it would be expected that these variables would prove significant in changes to a program with a more permanent authorization, such as Social Security. Social Security has been a hot-button issue for politicians for some time, with there being the need over time to modify the program. For example, in 1983, President Ronald Reagan signed legislation enacting changes to the Social Security program that were designed to increase the program's solvency. One might expect that these legislative changes were followed by a flurry of media coverage or of congressional hearings. However, as table 7.7 illustrates, this is not the case. Neither the hearings variable nor the media coverage variable achieves statistical significance, and their substantive significance in the model is minor as well. This analysis suggests that legislative activity in Congress is not occurring in the area of Social Security policy, because the Congress is holding hearings or the media are covering this issue. The model does not suggest what these other factors are, but the data do not suggest that media coverage or hearings are linked in this prominent case to legislative activity.

Summary

The macrolevel data presented in this chapter suggest that across the programs in question, short-term authorizations are a dominant force in

Table 7.7 Logistic Regression: Factors Influencing the Passage of
Legislation, Social Security Model

Variables	Coefficient	Standardized Coefficient	Standard Error	Significance
Hearings	0.574	1.775	1.565	0.714
Media Coverage	-0.002	0.998	0.037	0.952
Divided Congress	-0.174	0.84	1.267	0.891
Divided Government	0.146	1.157	1.09	0.893
Constant	0.22	1.246	2.28	0.923

$N = 25$
Log likelihood = 32.466
Negelkerke R^2 = 0.011

determining when policy change will occur. Legislation was most likely to be passed in the year when an authorization was set to expire. The correlations and the multivariate analyses both show the strength of the linkage between the expiration of an authorization and the passage of subsequent legislation. Additionally, it is important to note that hearings and media coverage also fail to hold sway over the enactment of legislation in the case of Social Security, a policy that does not have a short-term authorization.

These data strongly suggest that the Congress uses short-term authorizations to structure its political environment. Congress may take into account the information that they gain from hearings and from the happenings in the media, but these factors are not critical for determining when legislative action will occur. The problem with hearings is that Congress uses them often for informational purposes, but not necessarily at the time legislation is being considered. When Congress passed the No Child Left Behind Act, the only congressional hearings held were two markup hearings in the House. The Senate never even considered the bill in committee: the bill was immediately brought to the floor and amended, and then the two versions were resolved in conference. This law also illustrates the interesting role that media coverage plays in influencing policy. While there is some coverage of the actual debate over the law when the law is being passed, this coverage continues after the law passes. The media cover issues associated with the legislation's implementation—the difficulties that states and localities encounter. Again, this information is critical to Congress, but it does not drive legislative change.

8

The New Policy Environment

"Virtually all of my bill has been unauthorized. The Justice Department has not been reauthorized since I've been in Congress—almost 20 years. It makes my job triply difficult."
—Representative Harold Rogers (R-KY), Appropriations Committee Subcommittee Chairman.

In the previous chapters, the use of short-term authorizations as a control mechanism has been explored in depth. However, the utility of this mechanism in some policy areas is diminishing because certain committees are having a more and more difficult time successfully crafting reauthorization legislation. As the quote from Congressman Rogers emphasizes, the failure to reauthorize has effects across Congress and across the policy process more broadly, as members and other policy actors have to find other ways in which to change policy.

The origins of the deterioration of the reauthorization process may lie in the expansive use of this mechanism and in the deficit politics years of the 1980s. On the first point, the abundance of short-term authorizations allows Congress to evaluate how agencies are implementing federal programs, but they also increase the workload for congressional committees. This is especially true for programs operating with an annual authorization. These programs require a committee to hold hearings and then write new authorization legislation every year. Not surprisingly, these programs dominate the agenda of the relevant committee. The defense authorization, which is perhaps the most prominent annual authorization, is the only major piece of legislation the Armed Services Committees considers each year. Many committees use multiyear authorizations to minimize the costs associated with having to act to reauthorize these programs (LeLoup 1980). However, even committees with multiyear authorizations can have problems reauthorizing the programs under their control.

The second issue is that reauthorization politics often require money.

Figure 8.1 The Number of Programs with Expired Authorizations, 1990–1999

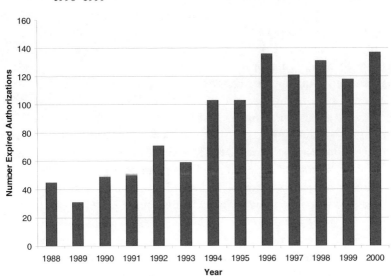

Oleszek (1989) argues that the influence of short-term authorizations on the budget and policy process is linked to the availability of funds to pay for these programs. When money is tight and deficits exist, the budgeters and the appropriators have most of the power. This makes being an authorizing committee member less important. One authorizing committee member summed up the situation by saying: "It's no fun being an authorization committee chairman anymore. They can't get new programs passed. The best they can do is preserve their most beloved programs at some level that makes sense" (Oleszek 1989, 76).

During the 1980s and early 1990s, authorization committees were forced to cut program funding, make them more efficient, and find ways of creating programs on the cheap. Beginning with the Reagan Administration, the use of the reconciliation process put the budget committees and the Appropriations Committees in the position of instructing authorizing committees to cut program and entitlement expenditures (Tiefer 1989). The budget deficits in the 1980s also made it harder for authorizing committees to build legislative coalitions and distribute program benefits to committee members.

Still, by the beginning of the 1990s there were relatively few programs that were operating with an expired authorization. According to the Congressional Budget Office (CBO 1990), 49 programs received appropriations with an expired authorization in 1990. By 1995 there had been a 110 percent increase in the number of programs receiving unauthorized appropriations, with 103 programs being expired but receiving appropriations (CBO 1995). Over this six-year period, the number of House committees with ten or more expired authorizations went from one to four, and, by the end of the decade, six House committees had ten or more expired authorizations that received appropriations. Figure 8.1 shows the change in the total number of unauthorized appropriations over the past decade.

The number of programs operating with expired authorizations varies across committees, with some committees—such as the Armed Services Committee—maintaining a business as usual approach to their annual defense authorization. However, other committees, such as the Commerce Committee, have seen a marked rise in the number of expired authorizations under their jurisdiction. This has led several observers to note that Congress no longer is doing its job. As Baumann (1999, 688) explains:

> While Congress likes to tackle such high-profile issues as tax cuts or military pay raises, one of Washington's dirty little secrets is that in many cases, lawmakers increasingly tend to neglect routine reauthorization bills for federal programs. The result: A myriad of programs are on automatic pilot because the House and Senate committees that have direct power over them have allowed their governing laws to expire.

Committees in Congress have always varied in their ability to pass legislation renewing the authorization of the programs under their jurisdiction that operate with a short-term authorization. Committees with large distributive programs, such as Public Works/Transportation and Infrastructure, Agriculture, and Armed Services, have traditionally been able to get their work done in a timely manner. With so many members reliant on the benefits of their work, these committees are able to craft coalitions and get their bills through both chambers. Typically, if one of these bills fails to be reauthorized in a timely manner, it is because committee members are fighting to increase the overall size of the program in order to have more money to distribute. This has been the case in the last four transportation authorizations, when the committees delayed producing a bill until the authorizers could secure the highest overall funding levels possible. Committees who handle regulatory issues, by contrast, often have more difficulty getting their programs reauthorized. In part, this is a function of the conflictive nature of the issues involved, and the level of conflict among the members of the committees involved.

In table 8.1, I examine the changes in unauthorized programs across House committees. The table shows that, in Fiscal Year 1990, there were only forty-nine programs operating with an expired authorization and 39

Table 8.1 Expired Authorizations by Committee, 1990–2000

	1990	1992	1994	1996	1998	2000	1990–92 Average	1996–2000 Average
Agriculture	1	4	3	2	3	4	2.5	3.0
Armed Services	1	1	2	3	0	1	1.0	1.3
Banking	2	4	4	4	4	5	3.0	4.3
Commerce	19	25	33	39	34	31	22.0	34.7
Education	5	6	5	13	20	12	5.5	15.0
Government Reform	2	—	4	6	2	4	2.0	4.0
Administration	1	1	1	—	1	1	1.0	1.0
Intelligence	—	—	—	0	1	1	—	0.7
International Relations	6	9	12	6	8	8	7.5	7.3
Judiciary	4	5	8	14	19	16	4.5	16.3
Resources	4	3	14	26	23	28	3.5	25.7
Science	5	8	8	13	13	15	6.5	13.7
Small Business	—	—	—	3	0	1	—	1.3
Transportation	4	6	9	15	10	15	5.0	13.3
Veterans' Affairs	—	—	4	6	2	3	—	3.7
Ways and Means	1	2	5	7	2	1	1.5	3.3
Merchant Marine	3	10	21	—	—	—	6.5	—
Post Office	—	1	2	—	—	—	1.0	—
Total (unduplicated)	49	71	103	136	131	137	60	134.7

Source: Unauthorized Appropriations and Expired Authorizations . This is an annual report of the
Congressional Budget Office that has been produced since 1985.
Note: The totals in each column do not equal the sum of the cells because some authorizations are assigned
to more than one committee.

percent of those programs were in one committee—Energy and
Commerce. In FY 1992 and FY 1994, the numbers slowly grew to total sev-
enty-one programs with unauthorized appropriations. Although the
Energy and Commerce Committee remained the largest offender with the
most unauthorized programs, its percentage of the overall number of
unauthorized appropriations actually declined slightly. Most committees
saw a slight rise in the number of unauthorized appropriations, but it was
the Merchant Marine and Fisheries Committee, a small, low conflict, nar-
row jurisdiction committee, that saw the total number of unauthorized
programming rise dramatically from three in FY 1990 to twenty-one in FY
1994. Two other committees—International Relations and Resources—
also saw the number of programs under their jurisdiction receiving appropriations without an authorization increase by a sizable number.

Since 1995, six House committees have had chronic problems addressing the short-term authorizations under their control. The Commerce
Committee and the Resources Committees are by far the most troubled.
The Commerce Committee has averaged having more than thirty-four
programs receive appropriations without authorization during the fiscal
years 1996 through 2000, and the Resources Committee has averaged having almost twenty-six programs per year operate without authorization.

Four other committees have averaged having more than ten programs annually receive appropriations without an authorization—Judiciary, Education, Science, and Transportation. One interesting feature in these data is that problems with reauthorizing programs permeate all types of committees. The problem with reauthorizing programs affects programs with highly fragmented jurisdictions (e.g., Commerce) and with very tight jurisdictions (e.g., Science). Committees with goals that are primarily constituent related (e.g., Resources) and policy oriented (e.g., Judiciary) have problems, as do committees that address issues with high (e.g., Education), medium (e.g., Transportation), and low (e.g., Science) issue salience.[1] Across the board, reauthorizations have become more problematic.

Why the Failure to Reauthorize?

Although the procedural explanation given in chapter 2 explains how unexpired authorizations get funded, it does not explain why committees cannot reauthorize programs in the first place. Two complementary reasons are generally offered for why Congress fails to reauthorize programs. One theory argues that committees fail to renew a short-term authorization because of high transaction costs associated with this action. The second theory argues that conflicts between the branches, or between the chambers in Congress, can cause the failure to reauthorize a program.

Cox (1996) notes that when committees use short-term authorizations as a means of controlling policy, it can cause them to have to pay high transaction costs. Specifically, when House and Senate committees make an authorization short-term, they put themselves in the position of having to reauthorize the legislation in the future, and assembling new legislative coalitions can be quite costly. Not only do the committees themselves have to agree on a policy when a program is reauthorized, but the committees then have to create floor coalitions that will support the reauthorization as well. Cox finds that committees sometimes realize when they create a new program that building legislative coalitions in the future will be extremely difficult, especially when the committee has no easy way to buy a coalition by distributing benefits among members. For example, when the bill to create the Occupational Safety and Health Administration (OSHA) was considered on the floors of the House and Senate, both authorizing committees lost control of the legislative process. The committees then worked to ensure that the new legislation made OSHA permanently authorized so that they did not have to consider this legislation in the future

The failure to act at any point in the legislative process means that the program will not be reauthorized, and there are numerous points in the legislative process, other than the committee stage and floor stage, where a bill can stall. Not surprisingly, as conflict between parties increases, and when the average level of conflict among committee members is higher, it is harder to reauthorize legislation. Cox finds that authorization committees that historically have high levels of conflict among members tend to use permanent authorization for agencies, as compared to committees with lower levels of internal conflict. Short-term authorizations come at the cost of having to enact new legislative coalitions when authorizations expire. When the costs of coalition creation and maintenance are too high, reauthorization efforts fail.

Krehbiel (1998) provides a slightly different argument about why legislation generally fails to be enacted. He points out that legislative efforts often fail because the preferences of the House, Senate, and president do not coincide. All three sets of stakeholders have to agree for a change in the status quo to occur; the new policy has to be better than existing policy for all three stakeholders. Krehbiel notes that efforts to develop a proposal that all three stakeholders will agree should be enacted are further hindered by two supermajoritarian procedures. First, at least sixty senators have to agree on a proposal for a filibuster to be prevented. Second, if the House and Senate want to act without the support of the president, two-thirds of both chambers have to support the proposal in order to overcome a veto by the president. Two examples highlight the problem identified by Krehbiel (1998). President Clinton's 1993 economic stimulus package was supported by a majority of senators and representatives. However, it was not enacted because of the supermajoritarian nature of the filibuster in the Senate; sixty senators did not support the proposal (Krehbiel 1998, 28–31). Similarly, supermajorities of the House and Senate supported the Family and Medical Leave Act in 1991, but these majorities were not large enough to overcome President Bush's veto of the bill; thus, the bill was not enacted (Krehbiel 1998, 31–33).

Krehbiel's (1998) argument is explicitly nonpartisan, but other scholars have suggested that partisan differences can make reauthorizations more difficult. Tiefer (1989) suggests that conflicts between the legislative chambers in the reauthorization process began in 1981, when Republicans took over control of the Senate. Senate Republicans were interested in enacting the initiatives of the Reagan Administration, preferably through permanent law. House Democrats, conversely, used the authorization process to critique and thwart the actions that Republicans were promoting. This form of intrabranch rivalry has been shown to be a major problem and an important cause of legislative inaction in recent years (Binder 1999).

Given the difficulty of crafting legislative agreements between the House, the Senate, and the president, the failure to reauthorize programs does not seem odd. Although there are gains in control over a program that occur with short-term authorizations, there are also procedural hurdles and transaction costs that must be overcome for a program to be reauthorized. In recent years, building legislative coalitions has become somewhat more difficult, especially since the Republicans took control of Congress. Richard Fenno (1997) has argued that the Republican takeover of the House resulted in highly inexperienced people being in charge of the chamber's operations. The lack of governing experience was complicated further by the large influx of inexperienced freshmen. Fenno notes (1997, 20):

> The governing expertise of which I speak is . . . expertise about the business of legislating. That business involves a practical grasp of lawmaking as a lengthy, incremental, multilevel, coalition-building process. And it involves a seasoned strategic sense in matters such as establishing priorities, negotiating outcomes across the separated institutions of government, and calculating feasibilities, trade-offs, and timing at every decisionmaking juncture. In short, successful governing takes a lot of practice, and the Republicans hadn't had any.

The regularized business of committees, of which the reauthorization of existing programs is a large and important part, was also affected by the way in which House Speaker Newt Gingrich (R-GA) organized the chamber after the Republican takeover. Fenno argues that Gingrich wanted to subordinate committee power to the power of the party's leadership. He did this by making a series of important changes to the existing committee system:

> The new Speaker abolished some committees and subcommittees, appointed the committee chairmen, extracted loyalty pledges from committee leaders, controlled committee staff, selected committee members, created and staffed ad hoc task forces to circumvent committees, established committee priorities and time lines, and monitored committee compliance. The end product was an American version of a prime minister in a system of party government and a legislative process with a lot less of the deliberative and incremental pacing that a committee-centered system can provide (Fenno 1997, 31).

The first two years of Republican control of Congress were also dominated by the bitter battles over federal appropriations. Because reauthorizations are often linked to the budget and appropriations processes—authorizing committees often want to maximize the benefits a program under their jurisdiction can provide—the uncertainty about the appropriations for Fiscal Year 1996 likely hindered the work of authorizers. It is clear that the debate over the budget dominated Washington and Congress for almost a year, eating up valuable time and resources that might otherwise have been used to revamp programs. The confrontation over the budget also serves to highlight the general clash of ideology and cultures that existed at the time between the House, Senate, and president. This clash made finding an ideal point for any policy more difficult, a factor that Krehbiel (1998) attributes to failures that occur generally in the legislative process.

The Policy Implications of Unauthorized Programs

There are also important policy implications that arise from a failure to reauthorize programs. As David Baumann (1999, 689) wrote in the *National Journal:*

> The consequence of [the failure to reauthorize programs] is increasingly poor congressional oversight over federal programs. Moreover, the annual congressional appropriations process gets bogged down in debates over controversial legislative issues that the authorizing committees of jurisdiction are supposed to deal with separately. Important policy issues that should be examined carefully and systematically are handled instead in the context of the appropriations bills, often during the frenzied final days of a legislative session.

When authorizing committees fail to reauthorize programs, the gains that Senator Russell pressed for when he moved the authorization for defense weapons systems acquisitions to a short-term authorization are lost. These committees cannot apply their subject matter expertise to the policy issue in question. They cannot provide effective ex ante oversight by changing the laws that underlie the program in question. And perhaps most detrimentally, authorizers end up ceding authority over the policy to appropriators and to the chamber as a whole, making appropriators the arbiters of policy. Several cases illustrate this point. First, Representative David Obey (D-WI) noted that

> when he chaired the Foreign Operations, Export Financing and Related Programs Appropriations Subcommittee, he added legislative language one year to his spending bill [affecting a program with an expired authorization], at the request of some authorizers—only to find out that

others [on the authorizing committee] opposed it. "All of a sudden, I was in
the middle of a shooting war with people on the authorizing committee."

The authorization for the National Endowment for the Arts (NEA) is
another case in point. The NEA was last authorized in 1990. Since that
time, there have been calls by many conservatives to terminate the program. However, Democrats and some Republicans in Congress continue to
support the program and its goals. Because the committee with jurisdiction has been unable to determine what should be done with the program,
it has fallen on the appropriations committees to be the arbiters of the program's status. House Appropriations Subcommittee Chairman Ralph
Regula (R-OH) recognizes that he is one of the people who get to make
almost all choices about arts funding and policy, even though it is not an
issue he cares about strongly. "To me, [adding legislative riders to the
appropriations bill is] just a matter of getting the bill out. I have no strong
feelings about the NEA one way or another, but I've had to [add riders
increasing the percentage of arts funds going directly to the states and
adding members of Congress to an NEA oversight group] to get my bills
through (Baumann 1999, 690).

The Education and the Workforce Committee had not addressed the
bill because the Committee chairman, William Goodling(R-PA), doubted
he could craft a coalition to support any revision to the law. With some
members wanting to kill the program, others wanting to modify it, and others wanting to keep it as is, finding the right balance of policy for a reauthorization bill has proven quite difficult. This impasse forces all interested
parties—legislators, interest groups, and the NEA itself—to use the appropriations process as the mechanism for making policy change to the program. The authorization process still occurs; it just occurs outside the
authorization committees, and appropriators, not authorizers, become the
final arbiters of the policy.

The change in congressional control has also had an impact on oversight
more broadly. Joel Aberbach's recent analysis (2001) finds that in the 1990s
there was a decline in the quality of oversight. However, the decline was not
in the amount of oversight conducted by congressional committees. When
oversight days for the first six months of the year are considered as a percentage of the total number of legislative days, the percentage of days allocated for oversight was similar across the three years. In fact, the
percentage of time devoted to oversight in the 1990s was roughly double
the amount that occurred in the 1970s, and sizably more than in the 1980s.

However, while the percentage of days dedicated to oversight has grown
dramatically in the 1990s, the total number of days is only slightly higher
than the number of hearing days held in the late 1970s and early 1980s. In

fact, the total number of hearing days in 1997 was the lowest since 1973. What accounts for the rise in the percentage of time being spent on oversight but not a rise in the absolute number of oversight days? Quite simply, congressional committees are in session far less than they have been in the past. In the 1970s and 1980s, the total number of committee days was never below 2,063; in the 1990s, the number never exceeded 1,483. In fact, committees met for 508 more days in 1961 than they did in 1997!

The result of this decline is that there are fewer committee days in which legislative work can be accomplished, and short-term authorizations have suffered as a result. Aberbach warns that the "decline in legislative activities, particularly reauthorizations and amendments, represents a serious decline in the amount . . . and quality, of oversight" (2001, 8), especially since legislative change is one of the most potent oversight tools in the congressional arsenal. Aberbach's view is supported by the comments of congressional leaders as well. As House Commerce Committee Chairman Thomas J. Bliley (R-VA) noted, in a busy legislative session, reauthorizing programs often takes a low priority. "Some of (the problem) is that Congress runs out of time. Committees feel there are other priorities. All of us start out every year saying we're going to do it, and then other events overtake us" (Baumann 1999, 691). Because committees meet for fewer days, they have to squeeze more legislative action into a shorter time frame, making the routine tasks more difficult to accomplish.

Summary

Over the past decade, there has been a marked rise in the number of programs operating with expired authorizations. This has been the result, in part, of a marked decline in the number of days in which congressional committees have met. Congress spends less and less time in committee, and this decline in the number of days has occurred roughly concomitantly with the rise in the number of programs with expired authorizations. The change in party control of Congress also resulted in one chamber of Congress having to learn an entirely new activity: governing. One result of this problem is that the policy process for many programs moved away from the authorizing committees and into the Appropriations Committees. Many appropriators found themselves with the job of attaching riders and approving policy for numerous programs that had been orphaned by authorizing committees. This abdication of responsibility made appropriations bills one of the key legislative vehicles for changing public policy.

9

Conclusion

Short-term authorizations have had a dramatic impact on the policy environment since their initial use after World War II. The original success of using short-term authorizations to control the policy implementation of the Marshall Plan showed that this new tool could be an effective mechanism for giving Congress greater control over how a policy was implemented. The subsequent passage of an amendment to put defense weapons procurement under a short-term authorization again put policy committees in the position of having greater control over how an agency implemented a specific program. Short-term authorizations added regularity to the process of reviewing defense procurement and strengthened the authorization committees with jurisdiction over it. Everyone involved in this policy area—members of Congress, lobbyists, and agency personnel—knew that there would be a bill addressing changes to defense procurement and knew when that bill would be considered by Congress.

With the Great Society came a great shift in the use of short-term authorizations. By the end of the 1960s, most new domestic programs—environmental regulations, education programs, economic development initiatives, agriculture programs, and transportation programs, to name just a few—were operating with short-term authorizations. These new programs were often more complex than the initial defense and foreign policy programs that utilized short-term authorizations. Now, the fifty states and a myriad of local governments, nonprofits, corporations, and federal agencies were often responsible for implementing a single program, instead of a single agency and a relatively small number of related stakeholders, as had been the case earlier (Hall and O'Toole 2000). This complexity made the ability to control the implementation of these programs and to modify their structure throughout the life of the program more important.

The Dynamics of Control

The issue of control has been emphasized throughout this book, and the cyclical nature of short-term authorizations and the dynamics of reauthorizations help to facilitate this. This control process begins with the writing of the initial legislation. As the Appalachian Regional Commission example from chapter 2 illustrated, the initial authorization designs the mechanism by which the program or agency will be controlled. It includes a variety of provisions that determine how the program is to function, the scope of its work, and the tools the actors involved in the implementation will have at its disposal.

By giving a program a short-term authorization at the outset, Congress ensures that the design of the program can be reconsidered in the future at a specified time. During the life of the authorization and through the reauthorization, three aspects of the control process come to the fore. The initial authorization locks down the time at which the law will be reconsidered and provides policy stability in the given area until the time for the reauthorization comes. By specifying this date, all policy actors know when the legislation will be renewed and can act accordingly. Congress can take the issue off of its agenda. Agency personnel and related interests involved with implementing the law can know that they have a specific period of time when the rules of the implementation game will remain relatively constant. Interest groups and all of the players affected by the program can also begin their efforts to shape the way in which the program is perceived and work to change the issue framing before the next reauthorization. This scheduling of the authorization also allows committees to tell these interests, some of whom were losers in the last policy battle, that they will not be changing the policy in question until the reauthorization. The stability that arises allows the agencies and others who are implementing the law to know that there will not be radical changes in the program in question. It also helps to ensure that the deals that members made during the reauthorization remain in place for the entire time of the authorization.

The time between authorizations is when Congress holds hearings that can shape the way in which the next authorization will play out. All of the factors that prominent policy scholars like Baumgartner and Jones (1993) and Sabatier and Jenkins-Smith (1993) have identified—the dynamics of advocacy frameworks, the role of media and hearings in shaping changes in the monopoly image of the program—are all occurring between reauthorizations. Congressional committees use these periods between authorizations for these informational purposes; they hold hearings throughout the life cycle of a program in order to capture information about how well the program is functioning, what changes should be made, and how various interest groups feel about the program as designed. The relatively consistent use of hearings over the life of a program helps congressional committees know how a program is functioning over time. It also provides a means for the experts within Congress, such as the General Accounting Office and the Congressional Budget Office, to bring information before the committee based on requested analyses.

The reauthorization itself is a key point when Congress can act to control agencies, control that comes from passing the reauthorization law. In the new reauthorization, Congress is in a position to reward or punish, to expand or contract the program, to give or take away agency discretion, to give or take away money as they reallocate funding formulas or distribute projects, and to expand or contract the number of organizations involved in the implementation of the program. In short, the law itself determines the future direction of the program and is the place where feedback that Congress receives from interest groups, agencies, constituents, the media, and others can be put to use in a way that directly affects policy.

In an interview, one lobbyist told me that "authorizations help committees schedule their lives."[1] The analysis in this book illustrates how short-term authorizations serve as a mechanism for controlling the timing of legislative activity in a given policy area. Legislative activity is in many ways controlled by the expiration of an authorization. When an authorization expires, it enhances the likelihood that legislation will be enacted in a given policy area. Between authorizations, there is little likelihood that there will be a change in the legislative basis for a given program or policy. Social Security provides an interesting case to illustrate the importance of short-term authorizations. For programs with short-term authorizations, legislative activity and a subsequent change in the law is largely predicated on the expiration of an authorization. In the case of Social Security, it is possible to see that other factors previously viewed as instigating policy change—the number of hearings on a topic and the amount of media coverage a program receives—provide little leverage for the passage of new legislation. With a short-term authorization, it is comparatively easy to predict when new legislation will be passed; without one, it is more difficult.

So what benefit does a committee gain from a short-term authorization? Predictability is one key benefit. The committee can control when the policy is open for debate and can ensure that the policy is not open for debate at other times. Most committees have many issues under their jurisdiction, and having short-term authorizations can help a committee control the flow of legislation from their committee. For example, the committees with jurisdiction over education make policy on several different education programs, including higher education, Head Start, vocational education, and primary and secondary education, and each one on a different reauthorization cycle. Short-term authorizations help the committees ensure that each policy is reviewed in a timely manner. They also allow committees to plan their schedules better so that these reviews are part of an overall structure of activities undertaken by the committee.

Stability is another benefit committees gain from using short-term authorizations. When committees use short-term authorizations, they know that the programs with one will typically not be disturbed prior to the expiration of the authorization. This mechanism allows committees to be confident that deals struck by committee members during the crafting of a bill will be honored for the duration of the legislation. For a committee to get any piece of legislation out and enacted into law, it must craft a bill that addresses the concerns of members of their own chamber and members of the other chamber. Compromises and deals have to be struck with a wide variety of interests to get a final product that can pass Congress.

Consider, for example, the compromises necessary to pass a surface transportation bill. Deals have to be struck on the formulas that allocate funds to states, on the cities that will receive transit new starts, on where projects of national significance will be designated, and on what regulations will or will not be included in the bill. As one former official of the U.S. Department of Transportation stated,

> Every time you do one of these bills, you are opening up Pandora's box, especially the battle over funding between donor states and donee states. Plus, you have the balance between the big four cities [Boston, Chicago, New York, and Washington, DC] that get all the transit money and everyone else. It is a nightmare."

The people who strike these deals want to know that the deal will not unravel unexpectedly. The fact that committees rarely revisit policy areas where they have recently crafted a short-term authorization allows all parties to feel confident that the deals that have been struck will remain in effect for the duration of the authorization.

Committees and members also benefit from the distributional and informational attributes of short-term authorizations. On the first point, there is a likely a reason why so many members of the House want to be on the Transportation and Infrastructure Committee, which is the largest committee in the House. This committee distributes more projects to member districts than any other committee, from road projects and transit new starts to airport improvements and coast guard services. Frances Lee (2003) has conducted some of the most highly sophisticated analyses of transportation policy making in the House. In her work, she shows how House members rarely can claim credit for much of the funding that flows to their constituents because funding formulas rarely, if ever, are designed to flow benefits to congressional districts. Instead, benefits flow to states or other political subdivisions. Reauthorizations are a time during which members can ensure that certain peculiar benefits flow to the member's district for which the member can claim credit.

Likewise, short-term authorizations allow a committee and its members to put their informational expertise to use in a meaningful way. Committees gather information about a program's effectiveness from a variety of sources, including formal mechanisms such as hearings or GAO reports and informal mechanisms such as constituent contacts or the media. The reauthorization process allows this information to be put to use as new legislation is crafted. The scheduling of this process ensures that information has time to be considered carefully and systematically. It also regularizes the opportunities that members have to engage in the electoral, political, and policy activities that make for a successful legislative career.

There are also benefits that accrue to the chamber as a whole, especially to the leaders of the House and Senate, from the use of short-term authorizations. One prominent benefit that is gained is predictability and efficiency in the scheduling of legislative activity. The legislative world is extremely complex, and the ability of Congress to finish even its most important work—the enactment of thirteen appropriations bills—has become quite difficult. Figure 9.1 shows the number of appropriations bills that had not been completed by the beginning of the new fiscal year for the 93rd through 103rd Congresses and the number of continuing resolutions that had to be passed in order to keep the government operating. Note that in only two Congresses were even *half* of all appropriations bills completed on time. In one Congress, no appropriations bills were completed on schedule; Congress batted zero for twenty-six in that two-year time span. Debate over these bills takes increasingly more time in Congress, leaving less time for Congress to debate substantive legislation from authorizing committees.

Now imagine a world where there was not a process for systematically reviewing legislation through short-term authorizations. Instead of a process in which Congress often moves into action and passes legislation on a policy when its authorization expires, legislation could move to the floor whenever there was an atypical number of legislative and nonlegislative hearings, an elevated level of media coverage of an issue, or new information that changed some aspect of the general understanding of the

Figure 9.1 Appropriations Bills Not Enacted and Continuing Resolutions Enacted, 93rd through 103rd Congresses

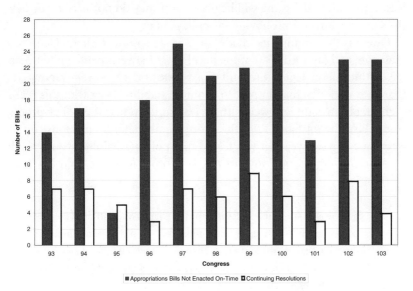

issue. In this environment, it would be difficult to craft legislation in the first place because members who were having their previous deals undone would likely protest, especially in the Senate, where the rules benefit the interests of members and of a minority of the chamber. However, the inadequacy of the deals might not be known initially. The whips would have to determine the level of support for every bill that was coming to the floor, and even worse, the majority leader in each chamber would have to make some effort to determine if the bills could even be scheduled, given completing demand.

Short-Term Authorizations: Normative Considerations

Short-term authorizations are not some sort of magic elixir that solves all problems. However, there is something beneficial that comes from a simple procedure that encourages periods of policy stability and also facilitates the regularized review of a policy and channels policy change into a fixed point in time. There are two normative arguments that can be made with regard to this type of benefit that accrues from short-term authorizations. First, there is a benefit that comes from understanding the impact of the law as crafted, and this knowledge typically comes only when stability is created in the policy environment. Second, by regularizing the times in which policy change will occur, the participants in the policy game all at least know when the game will begin, even if they do not necessarily have the same resources for lobbying for policy change.

One of the arguments made in *The Federalist Papers* (Hamilton, Madison, and Jay 1961) is that the new form of government would be stable. A bicameral legislature and the separation of powers among the branches were designed in part to promote stability. Even with this seemingly stable structure, however, there was concern that the policy process would be quite unstable. With the entire membership of the House up for election every two years, it was feared that policy instability would result. As Madison argues in *Federalist 62* (Hamilton, Madison, and Jay 1961, 380):

> Every new election in the States is found to change one half of the representatives. From this change of men must proceed a change of opinions; and from a change of opinions, a change of measures. *But a continual change of even good measures is inconsistent with every rule of prudence and every prospect of success.* (emphasis added)

The concern is that by making the United States a republican form of government, the change of personnel that accompanies the electoral process would give rise to wild swings in policy as new people with new ideas and opinions enter the government. Although change is not necessarily bad, Madison argues further (Hamilton, Madison, and Jay 1961, 381):

> The internal effects of a mutable policy are still more calamitous. It poisons the blessings of liberty itself. It will be of little avail to the people that the laws are made by men of their own choice if the laws are so voluminous that they cannot be read. . . . [I]f they be repealed or revised before they are promulgated, or undergo such incessant changes that no man, who knows what the law is today, can guess what it will be tomorrow. Law is defined to be a rule of action; but how can that be a rule, which is little known and less fixed.

Thus, what is needed for the public to have confidence in its government is to have both institutional stability and policy stability. Stability allows prudent people to plan their futures, to set a course for the future, and move deliberately forward knowing that the future is relatively clear. If the law is constantly changing, it becomes difficult to plan and to implement a policy. The instability undermines confidence in government and in the policy process. Madison notes that a person would be foolish to work in a constantly changing policy area because it would be impossible to know if the actions taken one day would be rational the next. For example, who would farm if the laws governing agriculture policy—laws covering subsidies, pesticides, export programs, and the like—changed every month? According to Madison, no reasonable person would be a farmer under such conditions. Policy stability promotes confidence that actions taken today will still seem rational tomorrow.

However, a different founder believed that too much stability was equally problematic as too little. Thomas Jefferson wrote on several occasions about his concern over whether "one generation of men has a right to bind another" to a set of laws or a form of government.[2] Jefferson did not oppose stability, but he was concerned about people being bound to a government that they had no say in developing. He argues "no society can make a perpetual constitution or even a perpetual law. The earth belongs always to the living generation" (Jefferson 1977, 449). Without the ability to change laws that need changing, the public is being ruled by a set of laws to which it did not consent, laws that were created by the dead. Jefferson notes that such a situation undermines confidence in government just as much as too little stability. In the latter case, people cannot trust government because its enactments are meaningless, but in the former case, the public is consigned to being ruled by laws it does not recognize as its own.

The short-term authorization process strikes a balance between these two positions. The short-term nature of the authorization ensures that policy can reflect the changes that occur in public opinion and in membership in the legislature. Thus, Jefferson's concern that no law be perpetual is addressed effectively. Likewise, Madison's concern about stability is addressed because the enactment of a short-term authorization helps to ensure that policy change does not occur between authorizations. By funneling the change Jefferson desires into specified points in time of which all are aware, the stability Madison so desires is achieved.

Regularizing the policy process with short-term authorizations also serves to create a more level playing field for interest group activity. Many scholars have noted that there is a bias in the policy process, with wealthy, well-organized interests (often corporate interests) dominating the process as they compete against smaller, less wealthy groups (often citizen interests). The difference in the wealth, organization, membership, or connections capacities among groups can allow some groups to have a greater say in the policy process than others.[3] Obviously, short-term authorizations do nothing to change the capacities of different interest groups. However, they do serve to ensure that all groups know when major policy debates will occur. Small interest groups can horde their resources between reauthorizations with relative certainty that major changes in policy will not occur. These groups can then have the resources they need to make their case to Congress when the legislation is considered again. By creating a process when everyone knows that the windows will open at a specific time, people know when new policies will be trying to sneak in and can plan accordingly.

Rethinking the Policy World

The use of short-term authorizations allows the policy process to be regularized and made predictable. The process of considering policy change in a larger process that includes the legislative process, implementation, and evaluation, with the process then repeating, resembles the policy stages that have long been critiqued by various scholars (e.g., Sabatier 1999). However, certain institutional actors, like the Congress, have incentives to keep the policy process as simple as possible, and using short-term authorizations brings a certain level of predictability and stability to the policy process.

Adler and Wilkerson (2003) found in studying bill introductions that short-term authorizations bridge across traditional conceptions of how the policy process works. They note:

> Public policy agenda setting research seeks to attribute such variations in policy attention to external events (e.g., 9/11) that focus attention on an issue or lead legislators to redefine and revisit existing issues (Baumgartner and Jones 1993). Institutionalists seek to explain policy priorities and legislative progress (or the absence or it) in terms of preferences and the impact of decision rules on which preferences matter most (Krehbiel 1998; Shepsle and Weingast 1981) . . . Authorization sunsets are an important predictor of when legislators will become interested and active in a policy area. . . . [F]ailing to account for authorization schedules can lead to biased estimates of the importance of other causal relationships. In some cases, the consequence will be to attribute more importance to a different variable than is deserved [or] . . . too little importance to a variable than is deserved. [For example,] knowing that a program is or is not up for reauthorization can also help to explain why a defining election leads to policy change in one policy but not in another. (14–15)

The authorization process affects agencies, interest groups, Congress, and the president, and as the quote above notes, this simple mechanism may affect how certain aspects of the legislative process, and policy process more broadly, are understood. This policy mechanism needs to be studied more thoroughly so that the federal policy process can be understood more completely.

Methodological Appendix

Studying the policy process in Congress has always required trade-offs. Because Congress is such a vast institution with two chambers that have more than a dozen committees in each, scholars have to make critical decisions about how to design research examining the institution. The first issue scholars typically have to consider is whether to examine the policy process in both chambers or whether to examine it in only one, typically the House of Representatives. Because this analysis focuses primarily on policy outcomes, this issue is of less importance to my design. I do use House hearings as an independent variable in the analysis; however, recent scholarship by Andrew Taylor (2001) shows that oversight patterns in the House and Senate are similar, suggesting that including hearing data from only one chamber is not problematic.

Once the decision is made about which chamber(s) to study, it is then necessary to decide whether to examine all committees in the institution or examine specific committees that can be viewed as being representative of one chamber and then extrapolate from this smaller sample. Finally, it is necessary to determine what specific policies are to be studied, the scope of the policy to be studied, and the way various key variables in the study are to be defined. So a scholar might ask, if I am going to study education policy, should I examine education policy broadly, or the Elementary and Secondary Education Act specifically? How do I know when activities such as changes in the policy occur? What time frame should be used to study the policy process in question?

Studying short-term authorizations in Congress requires considering these same factors. Scholars of Congress and public policy each tend to study slices of the whole, not the whole itself. It is very difficult to study all committees in Congress, just as it is difficult to study all policy domains. Fortunately, there are clear strategies for leveraging existing knowledge about Congress and the policy process in order to be able to develop findings that are broadly meaningful. One strategy is to examine a single issue, committee, or policy in great depth, typically over a long period of time, in order to determine the dynamics of the given situation, and then attempt to make broader conclusions from this case. Mark Hansen's (1991) study of the evolution of farm lobby access in Congress from 1919–81 is a case in point.

Here, Hansen uses one policy area—agriculture—and two committees, the House and Senate Agriculture Committees, to make a powerful argument regarding the factors that lead to farming interests gaining and losing power within Congress. David King (1996) used a similar technique to study changes in committee jurisdictions and bill referrals in the House. Although his study has larger implications, King focuses his work almost exclusively on the then-named House Energy and Commerce Committee. In the policy studies literature there have been many analyses that focused on a single case. The implementation literature has often examined a specific policy or program, starting with Pressman and Wildavsky's *Implementation* (1973). Likewise, the tests of the Advocacy Coalition Framework have typically focused on single policy domains (Sabatier and Jenkins-Smith 1993).

The alternate technique that scholars have used is to study a small sample over a shorter, but still relatively long, time frame. The goal of this research design is to increase the number of cases studied in order to expand the explanatory power of the theory, so that it can be generalized beyond the specific cases in question. In the congressional literature, Richard Fenno's *Congressmen in Committees* (1973) is a classic example. He studied five House committees and the corresponding six Senate committees over a twelve-year time frame to test "the assumption . . . that congressional committees matter [and] the theme . . . that congressional committees differ" (1973, xiii). Fenno sampled across committees in order to understand powerful committees, such as Ways and Means, as well as the much less powerful, such as Post Office and Civil Service. Heinz and his colleagues (1993) applied this tactic to studying the role of private interests in the federal policy process. Their work focuses on four policy domains—agriculture, energy, health, and labor—but they are able to draw broader conclusions from their work. In the policy literature Kingdon (1995) and Baumgartner and Jones (1993) both study a small number of policy areas in order to test their respective theories. Kingdon focused on studying transportation and health policy, and Baumgartner and Jones used a variety of cases, including nuclear power, pesticides, smoking, and drug use, in their work.

In general, the scholars conducting these studies have not claimed that the analyses are perfect experimental or quasi-experimental designs; the topics or committees being studied were not randomly selected. Typically, the studies use a stratified sample, as is the case with Fenno's work, so that there can be generalizations made across a range of situations, but these stratified samples are still self-selected by the authors for various reasons, including data availability or because the topics in question are of broader interest.

In this study, I use a research design similar to that of Fenno and Baumgartner and Jones in that I test how short-term authorizations impact the policy process across several policy domains over a relatively long, twenty-five-year time frame. For most of the analyses, I focus on three domains that use short-term authorizations—education policy, transportation policy, and regulatory policy. I also examine Social Security as a control case, because it is a permanent program. For each policy area that uses short-term authorizations, I then selected four programs for closer study. The purpose for this is straightforward: Congress generally does not pass laws about policy domains; they pass laws that create or modify programs. Instead of passing laws about early childhood education, Congress enacts legislation related to Head Start or the Elementary and Secondary Education Act. Therefore, the study focuses on legislation that emerges from Congress, an issue that I will discuss in more detail later in this chapter.

There are two time frames for the data included in the analysis. For the budgeting and appropriations data included in chapter 4, the fiscal years 1977 through 1994 are used. The data begin in FY 1977 because that is the year in which the beginning of the federal fiscal year moved from July 1 to October 1. Additionally, other aspects of the Congressional Budget and Impoundment Control Act of 1974 were fully implemented by FY 1977. The data on oversight and agenda setting include the years 1970 through 1994, which provides a twenty-five-year time frame in which to consider the impact of short-term authorizations on policy change. The one limitation of this time frame is that it does not reflect the dynamics of the policy process under Republican control of Congress, which began in January 1995. However, I do discuss how short-term authorizations have changed under Republican control in chapter 8.

The policy domains selected for this analysis were chosen with an interest in creating a meaningfully stratified set of cases. Thus, the policies and programs included in the analysis were selected based upon different characteristics. First, I attempted to select policy areas that are well defined and that fit generally within the jurisdiction of a single committee. By doing so, I can examine issues associated with temporary authorizations—especially oversight and agenda setting—in a clearer manner. Additionally, I can leverage the research of scholars of committees to ensure that there is diversity in the environments in which various policies are considered. Drawing on the work of several scholars, I used the following factors to differentiate between committees: (1) fragmentation, (2) salience, (3) conflict, (4) committee goals, (5) external effects, (6) outlier status, and (7) average number of unauthorized appropriations, 1990–99. Each factor is discussed below.

Fragmentation considers the breadth of a committee's jurisdiction. Two factors—the number of departments and agencies that are under the committee's jurisdiction, and the number of issues listed in the chamber's rules—are used to measure fragmentation. The importance of fragmentation is that it "considers the degree to which a committee attracts the attention of outsiders who perceive their interests as unrelated to each other" (Smith and Deering 1990, 77). The more issues a committee has to consider, the greater the number of different outside interests acting to pressure the committee.

Salience takes into account the importance with which the public and members of Congress view the issues within a committee's jurisdiction. An issue's salience is in part based on how many people it affects. For instance, Social Security is a high salience issue because it affects all Americans. Salience can be measured by considering the amount of news coverage an issue receives (Smith and Deering 1990, 78–85).

Conflict considers the level of competition between interest groups who have issues before a committee. The higher the level of conflict, the more members must choose between the interests of one group of actors to the exclusion of the interests of other groups of actors. Members often find high levels of conflict to be problematic politically, because, as then Congressman Richard Durbin (D-IL) noted, it requires members "to vote . . . on matters that make people unhappy" (Smith and Deering 1990, 84).

Committee goals come from Fenno (1973), who identified three goals that members desire to achieve when they serve on a committee: reelection, good public policy, and influence within the chamber. Smith and Deering (1990) quantified Fenno's work by surveying members and member staff regarding which committees they viewed as being most appealing. Through the survey, it was possible to determine which committees were viewed as prestigious, as policy driven, or as constituency driven (Smith and Deering 1990, 85–90).[1]

External effects consider how the average policy produced by agencies under a committee's jurisdiction affect members who are not on the committee. If a committee has uniform externalities, the average policy affects all noncommittee members equally. The Appropriations Committee is an example of one with uniform externalities. If a committee has targeted externalities, the average policy tends to affect significantly a limited number of noncommittee members. Resources, the House committee that handles federal lands, has targeted externalities. Committees that do not fall in either category are considered to have mixed externalities. The Judiciary Committee is an example of a committee with mixed externalities (Cox and McCubbins 1993, 191–202).

Outlier status considers if the membership of a legislative committee is dominated by members with policy preferences that are extreme compared to the average member of the House. Because individual members have, to a limited extent, the opportunity to self-select onto committees, some scholars argue that committees are composed of individuals who have a high demand for the policies that a committee produces (Shepsle 1978; cf. Cox and McCubbins 1993). For example, members on the

Table A.1   Characteristics of House Committees

Committee	Fragmentation	Salience	Conflict	Goals	External Effects	Outlier Status[1]
Agriculture	Medium	Low	Low	Constituent	Targeted	Nonoutlier
Appropriations	High	Medium	Medium	Prestige	Uniform	Nonoutlier
Armed Services	Medium	Medium	Medium	Constituent	Mixed	Outlier
Banking	Medium	Medium	Medium	Policy	Mixed	Nonoutlier
Budget	—	High	High	Prestige	—	Nonoutlier
Commerce	High	High	High	Policy	Uniform	Nonoutlier
Education	High	High	High	Policy	Mixed	Outlier
Government Operations	Medium	Low	Low	Policy	Uniform	Nonoutlier
International Relations	High	High	Medium	Policy	Mixed	Outlier
Judiciary	High	High	High	Policy	Mixed	Nonoutlier
Resources	High	Medium	Medium	Constituent	Targeted	Nonoutlier
Science	Low	Low	Low	Constituent	Uniform	Nonoutlier
Transportation	High	Medium	Medium	Constituent	Uniform	Nonoutlier
Veterans	Low	Low	Low	Constituent	Uniform	Nonoutlier
Ways and Means	Low	Medium	High	Prestige	Uniform	Nonoutlier

[1]Krehbiel (1993) finds that when using interest group scores, only one committee, the Armed Services Committee, was composed of "high demanders." In this table, I use Krehbiel's findings (1993, 128–30) regarding the general ideology of committee members.

Agriculture Committee want more agriculture policy than the average House Member. The outlier status of a committee's members can be measured through the use of interest group scores and ideology scores.

Table A.1 shows how committees rank based upon these six factors. For the analysis of budgeting and appropriations conducted in chapter 4, six policy areas are included in the analysis: (1) agriculture, (2) armed services, (3) regulatory/commerce, (4) education, (5) international relations, and (6) transportation. For chapters 5, 6, and 7 almost all of the analysis focuses on regulatory/commerce, education, transportation, and defense policies, with Social Security policy used as a control case. The committees that have primary jurisdiction over these policy areas vary across the factors noted above. There are committees with high and medium levels of fragmentation, and committees with high, medium, and low levels of conflict and issue salience. Both policy and constituent committees are represented in the data. Committees with targeted, uniform, and mixed externalities also are represented. These committees also vary regarding how well their membership reflects the ideology of the average member on the floor.

These committees also vary in the likelihood that they will reauthorize programs in a timely manner and in the typical length of authorizations under their jurisdiction. During the period analyzed in this study, three of the committees—Agriculture, Armed Services, and International Relations—had relatively few programs under their jurisdiction functioning with expired authorizations. Two committees—Education and the Workforce and Transportation and Infrastructure—had a moderate number of programs operating with expired authorizations. And one committee in the study—the Commerce Committee—ranks as the committee with the most programs operating with expired authorizations.

After selecting the policy areas, I then select for some of the programs a set of subcategories that fit within these policy areas. For example, for education policy, I examine early childhood education, special education, vocational education, and arts and humanities funding. By examining these subcategories, I am better able to consider how Congress makes policy in a more meaningful way, since congressional activity rarely focuses on a broad policy, like education or health care, but instead is more focused on a slice of that policy, like special education or health insurance. Most issues are too large to be considered en banc, so instead they are broken into smaller, more meaningful components. As one congressional staff person noted to me, "Every time we do an authorization, we produce a huge bill. The last one was several hundred pages. You cannot combine this issue with another one. We can only handle doing one at a time." For the regulatory programs included in the analysis, it was not necessary to divide the policies into programs, but for education and transportation, I consider programmatic aspects of these policies.

Using the Agendas Project Data

Many of the data used in this book come from the Policy Agendas Project.[2] This project provides comprehensive data on all hearing activity in Congress and all public laws passed in the postwar period. The data are coded by topics and subtopics, which allows scholars to search for information about specific policies or programs. The data sets that were used in chapters 4, 5, and 7 were constructed by searching through specific subtopics for information

Table A.2   Policy Agenda Project Subtopics Used, by Program

Education	Subtopic
Disability Education	606
Head Start	603
National Endowment for the Arts	609
Vocational Education	604
Regulatory	**Subtopic**
Commodity Futures Trading Commission	1502
Consumer Product Safety Commission	1525
Nuclear Regulatory Commission	801, 501
Securities and Exchange Commission	1502
Transportation	**Subtopic**
Amtrak	1005
Coast Guard	1007
Federal Aviation Administration	1003
Mass Transit	1001
Social Security	**Subtopic**
Social Security	1300, 1303

about these programs. For example, subtopic 603 (Education of Underprivileged Students) was used to create the data set information related to Head Start. Because the subtopic categories are the same for public laws and hearings, it is possible to combine the public law and hearing components of the Policy Agendas Project data together by year to get an overall picture of activity in a certain policy area or for a certain program. Table A.2 shows the topic codes from which the data used in this analysis were obtained. I was able to use these data as an initial roadmap for learning about each program, which I then supplemented with data about media coverage and data about the laws themselves, which can be obtained from the United States Code Congressional and Administrative News (USCCAN), which contains the text of every law passed by Congress.

Statistical Notes

The data for each time series used in chapter 7 were analyzed in three ways. First, the data were entered and pooled to allow for a pooled cross-sectional time series analysis across all programs. Pooling allows for the observation of variation of appropriations over time and increases the total number of observations (N) of the data set. With twelve programs examined over twenty-five years, pooling increases the N for the data set twelve-fold. There are several statistical assumptions that must be addressed in a pooled time series analysis, including autoregression, autocorrelation, and heteroscedasticity (Sayrs, 1989). The presence of any of these can result in biased and unreliable statistical outcomes. The most effective means of testing these problems is to create a fixed effects model (Greene 1997; Kennedy 1998), controlling for both the cross sections and the time series corrections for dependencies in the data (Beck, Katz, and Tucker, 1997).

Second, the data were analyzed by policy area using cross-sectional time series analysis, with data for each program entered by year, and then pooled with data for other similar programs. This gave an N for each policy area totaling 100, except for Social Security ($N = 25$). A binary logistic regression model was used to test the hypotheses, with the dependent variable being whether legislation was enacted in a given year or not. It would be possible also to analyze these data using OLS regression, with the dependent variable being the number of legislative enactments passed in a given year. However, this variable is highly bounded; its value never exceeds five and in 91 percent of the cases the value is zero, one, or two. I therefore transformed the dependent variable into a simple dichotomous variable that equals zero if no legislative action occurred related to the program in question and equals one if legislative action occurred. This transformation made using a logistic regression the preferred method of analysis (Menard 1995).

Third, the data were analyzed by program instead of by policy, and, instead of using a dichotomous dependent variable, I use the number of bills passed in each year. As was noted above, this dependent variable is highly bounded; between zero and five. In such a case, a Poisson regression—which estimates the maximum likelihood models of the number of occurrences (counts) of an event over time—can be employed to examine changes in the model. In this analysis, the change that is being examined is in the lawmaking that is occurring over time.

Notes

Chapter 1

1. There is a very large literature on each point made in paragraph 1 of this chapter. However, Mayhew (1991) has done much to show that partisanship does not necessarily interfere with the production of legislation.

2. Interview with a former transportation committee staffer, February 20, 2002. This interview, and all subsequent interviews noted, was conducted by the author. The interviews were conducted under rules of my project approval by the Human Subjects Office, Office of the Vice President of Research, University of Georgia. This approval included a stipulation that I would provide all interview subjects with anonymity for agreeing to submit to an interview.

Chapter 2

1. U.S. Code Congressional and Administrative News. 1965. 1: 6.

2. U.S. Code Congressional and Administrative News. 1965. 1: 22.

3. Taken from the Congressional Record, page H5747, July 24, 1991. http://thomas.loc.gov/cgi-bin/query/D?r102:1:./temp/~r102dK58g0:: accessed July 19, 2001.

4. Taken from the Congressional Record, page H5747, July 24, 1991. http://thomas.loc.gov/cgi-bin/query/D?r102:1:./temp/~r102dK58g0:: accessed July 19, 2001.

5. Shepsle and Weingast (1987a and 1987b) have argued that committees are powerful because they have an ex post veto over actions taken by the floor (cf. Krehbiel 1987). This ex post veto is exercised when legislation goes to a conference committee, and committee members responsible for the bill are disproportionally represented on conference committees and can veto changes made on the floor to their bill.

6. As quoted from Compilation of the Legislative Reorganization Act of 1946. S. Doc. 71, 26.

Chapter 3

1. As Shepsle and Bonchek (1997, 327) note, "exclusive gatekeeping authority [makes it] practically impossible for the full legislature to consider changes in the status quo in a committee's jurisdiction unless the committee consents to open the gates. This makes a committee an agenda monopolist in its jurisdiction."

2. The argument made in this section is not contingent on committees being composed of preference outliers (e.g., Shepsle 1978; Weingast and Marshall 1988) or being more heterogeneous in preferences (e.g., Hall and Grofman 1990; Krehbiel 1990, 1991). It is interesting to note, however, that committees are limited in size and there are trade-offs in making them larger (e.g., Munger 1988). In the 105th Congress, almost 20% of the House was on the Transportation and Infrastructure Committee.

3. Interview with senior manager in the U.S. Department of Education, February 2002.

4. Interview with a congressional staff person who has served on the Education and the Workforce Committee, February 2002.

Chapter 4

1. From an interview with a person who has been involved in transportation policy and lobbying, February 18, 2002.

2. The Coast Guard and the Nuclear Regulatory Commission both had an annual authorization prior to 1980.

Chapter 5

1. As quoted from Compilation of the Legislative Reorganization Act of 1946. S. Doc. 71, 26.

2. Art (1985, 235), with the original quote coming from the National Journal, March 13, 1984: 614.

3. More information about the methodology used in this analysis can be found in the Methodological Appendix.

Chapter 7

1. Interview with Department of Education staff person, February 2002.

2. Interview with a congressional staff person who has served on the Education and the Workforce Committee, February 2002.

3. Media coverage was determined by using the Reader's Guide. The topical headings for each program remained constant over time.

4. In the model shown in table 7.2, the values in the far right column are computed when all variables are held at their mean. Because there are several dummy variables in the model, it is also beneficial to examine the impact of each independent variable on the likelihood that a new law will pass when all other dummy variables were held at either zero or one. Dr. Paul R. Hensel has created "an Excel program that allows the user to calculate expected values from a logistic regression model . . . and [provides] overall expected values for the model as well as changes in the expected values when moving from one value of each variable to another" (http://garnet.acns.fsu.edu/~phensel/Data/logit.xls, last accessed, September 28, 2003). Using this tool, it is possible to calculate the probability of a law being passed if each dummy variable is held at either zero or one. This creates six possible conditions—a divided or unified government, a divided or unified Congress, and an authorization year or off year, and it is possible to examine the impact of each independent variable on the likelihood of a legislative enactment occurring. These results show that the hearings and media coverage variables at most increase the likelihood that a law will pass by 14 percent. The expiration of authorization variable increases the likelihood that a law will pass by approximately 70 percent over all possible combinations.

5. Again, if I examine the six scenarios created by holding the dummy variables at zero or one, I find that when the hearings and media coverage variables move from one standard deviation below the mean to one standard deviation above the mean, it increases the likelihood that a law will pass by 13 percentage points or less. The expiration of an authorization increases the likelihood that a law will pass by 78 percentage points across all scenarios.

6. Interview with Department of Education staff person, February 2002.

7. Interview with Education and the Workforce Committee staffer, February 2002.

8. Interview with Department of Education staff person, February 2002.

9. If I calculate the probability of a transportation law being passed if each dummy variable is held at either zero or one, we find that the hearings variable increases the likelihood that a law will pass by at most 25%, and the media variable peaks at less than 10%. This analysis shows that the expiration of authorization variable is again the dominant variable, increasing the likelihood that a law will pass by between 51% and 78%.

10. Interview with former state transportation official conducted February 18, 2002.

11. Interview with a former transportation committee staffer, interviewed on February 20, 2002.

12. When I calculate the impact of changes in each independent variable on the likelihood that a law will pass, I find that, when all other variables are held constant, increases in the number of hearings had no impact on the likelihood

that a law will pass. The media coverage variable results, at most, in a 20% increased likelihood of a law passing. However, the program's authorization status increases the likelihood a law will pass by between 45% and 51%.

13. Interview with staff person of a regulatory agency included in the analysis, conducted on February 19, 2002.

Chapter 8

1. The Methodological Appendix contains additional information about how each House committee ranks across these various characteristics.

Chapter 9

1. As quoted by a former appropriations staffer who now works as a lobbyist, February 19, 2002.

2. This quote is from a letter Jefferson wrote to James Madison in 1789 (Jefferson 1977, 445). He made a similar argument in a letter to Samuel Kercheval in 1816 (Jefferson 1977, 552–561).

3. A comprehensive review of this literature can be found in Frank K. Baumgartner and Beth L. Leech's book *Basic Interests: The Importance of Groups in Politics and in Political Science* (1998), especially chapters 5 and 6.

Methodological Appendix

1. Constituency committees reflect the re-election considerations mentioned by Fenno. Additionally, several committees, such as the Ethics Committee, were not requested, but the committees in this category are also not authorizing committees as traditionally defined (Smith and Deering 1990, 85–90).

2. The data used here were originally collected by Frank R. Baumgartner and Bryan D. Jones, with the support of National Science Foundation (NSF) grant number SBR 9320922, and were distributed through the Center for American Politics and Public Policy at the University of Washington and/or the Department of Political Science at Pennsylvania State University. Neither NSF nor the original collectors of the data bear any responsibility for the analysis reported here. All of the data for the project can be found at http://www.policyagendas.org.

References

Aberbach, Joel D. 2001. "Republican Oversight." Presented at the 2001 Midwest Political Science Association Meeting in Chicago, IL.

―――. 1990. *Keeping a Watchful Eye: The Politics of Congressional Oversight.* Washington, DC: The Brookings Institution

―――. 1979. "Changes in Congressional Oversight." *American Behavioral Scientist* 22: 493–515.

Ainsworth, Scott. 1997. "The Role of Legislation in the Determination of Interest Group Influence in Legislatures." *Legislative Studies Quarterly* 22: 517–34.

―――. 1993. "Regulating Lobbyists and Interest Group Influence." *The Journal of Politics* 55, 1: 41–56.

Art, Robert J. 1989. "The Pentagon: The Case for Biennial Budgeting." *Political Science Quarterly* 104, 2: 193–214.

―――. 1985. "Congress and the Defense Budget: Enhancing Policy Oversight." *Political Science Quarterly* 100, 2: 227–48.

Balla, Steven J. 1998. "Administrative Procedures and Political Control of the Bureaucracy." *American Political Science Review* 92, 3. (Sept., 1998): 663–73.

Balla, Steven J. and Christopher J. Deering. 2001. "Oversight over Time and across Committees: An Operational Measure of Police Patrols and Fire Alarms." Presented at the 2001 Midwest Political Science Association Meeting in Chicago, IL.

Banks, Jeffrey S. 1989. "Agency Budgets, Cost Information, and Auditing." *American Journal of Political Science,* 33, 3: 670–99.

Banks, Jeffrey S. and Barry R. Weingast. 1992. "The Political Control of Bureaucracies under Asymmetric Information." *American Journal of Political Science* 36, 2: 509–24.

Bauer, Raymond A., Ithiel de Sola Pool, and Lewis Anthony Dexter. 1972. *American Business & Public Policy: The Politics of Foreign Trade.* 2nd ed. Chicago: Aldine–Atherton.

Baumann, David. 1999. "Government on Autopilot." *The National Journal* (March 13): 688–92.

Baumgartner, Frank R. and Bryan D. Jones. 1993. *Agendas and Instability in American Politics.* Chicago: University of Chicago Press.

Baumgartner, Frank R. and Beth L. Leech. 1998. *Basic Interests: The Importance of Groups in Politics and in Political Science.* Princeton: Princeton University Press.

Beck, Nathaniel, Jonathan N. Katz, and Richard Tucker. 1997. "Taking Time Seriously: Time-Series Cross-Section Analysis with a Binary Dependent Variable." *American Journal of Political Science* 42, 4: 1260–88.

Bendor, Jonathan and Terry M. Moe. 1986. "Agenda Control, Committee Capture, and the Dynamics of Institutional Politics." *American Political Science Review* 80, 4: 1187–1207.

Berry, Jeffrey M. 2000. *The New Liberalism: The Rising Power of Citizen Groups.* Washington, DC: Brookings Institution Press.

Binder, Sarah A. 1999. "The Dynamics of Legislative Gridlock." *American Political Science Review* 93, 3: 519–34.

Birnbaum, Jeffrey. 1987. *Showdown at Gucci Gulch.* New York: Random House.

Bond, Jon R. and Richard Fleisher. 1990. *The President in the Legislative Arena.* Chicago: University of Chicago Press.

Brady, David and Barbara Sinclair. 1984. "Building Majorities for Policy Changes in the House of Representatives." *Journal of Politics* 46, 4: 1033–60.

Browne, William P. and Won K. Paik. 1993. "Beyond the Domain: Recasting Network Politics in the Postreform Congress." *American Journal of Political Science* 37, 4: 1054–78.

Burkhead, Jesse. 1956. *Government Budgeting.* New York: John Wiley & Sons.

Caiden, Naomi. 1983. "Guidelines to Federal Budget Reform." *Public Budgeting & Finance* 3: 4–22.

Calderia, Gregory A. and John R. Wright. 1990. "Amici Curiae before the Supreme Court: Who Participates, When, and How Much?" *The Journal of Politics* 52, 3: 782–806.

———. 1988. "Organized Interests and Agenda Setting in the U.S. Supreme Court." *American Political Science Review* 82, 4: 1109–27.

Cohen, Jeffrey E. 1995. "Presidential Rhetoric and the Public Agenda." *American Journal of Political Science* 39: 87–107.

Collender, Stanley E. 1997. *The Guide to the Federal Budget: Fiscal Year 1997.* Lanham, MD: Rowman & Littlefield Publishers.

Committee on the Budget. 1997. *The Congressional Budget Process: An Explanation.* Washington, DC: United States Senate. Committee Print: 104–70.

Congressional Budget Office. 1990–2000. *Unauthorized Appropriations and Expiring Authorizations.* Washington, DC: The Congress of the United States.

Congressional Quarterly Almanac. 1998a. "Dispute over Competition Leads to Interim Six-Month Reauthorization of FAA." 24–34–24–35.

Congressional Quarterly Almanac. 1998b. "Transportation Law Benefits Those Who Held the Purse Strings." 24–3–24–12.

Congressional Quarterly Almanac. 1994a. "FAA Reauthorized for Three Years." 168–69.

Congressional Quarterly Almanac. 1994b. "Lawmakers Renew and Revamp 1965 Education Act." 383–96.

Congressional Quarterly Almanac. 1993. "Transportation Programs Score Big Gains." 663–70.

Congressional Quarterly Almanac. 1991. "Air Bag Mandates Moved." 15.

Congressional Quarterly Almanac. 1988. "Consumer Product Safety." 580–81.

Congressional Quarterly Almanac. 1977. "How Wright Fashioned His Victory." 6.

Cook, Brain J. 1989. "Principal-Agent Models of Political Control of Bureaucracy." *American Political Science Review* 83, 3: 965–78.

Cox, Gary W. and Mathew D. McCubbins. 1993. *Legislative Leviathan: Party Government in the House.* Berkeley: University of California Press.

Cox, James Harrington. 1996. *Struggling with Control without Losing Control: Congressional Use of Temporary Authorization to Control Bureaucratic Implementation.* Dissertation: University of North Carolina at Chapel Hill.

Dawson, Raymond H. 1962. "Congressional Innovation and Intervention in Defense Policy: Legislative Authorization of Weapons Systems." *The American Political Science Review* 56, 1: 42–57.

Deering, Christopher J. and Steven S. Smith. 1997. *Committees in Congress.* 3rd ed. Washington, DC: CQ Press.

Denzau, Arthur T. and Robert J. Mackay. 1983. "Gatekeeping and Monopoly Power of Committees: An Analysis of Sincere and Sophisticated Behavior." *American Journal of Political Science* 27, 4: 740–61.

Diermeier, Daniel and Timothy J. Federsen. 2000. "Information and Congressional Hearings." *American Journal of Political Science* 44, 1: 51–65.

Dodd, Lawrence C. and Richard L. Schott. 1979. *Congress and the Administrative State.* New York: John Wiley & Sons.

Downs, Anthony. 1972. "Up and Down with Ecology: The Issue Attention Cycle. *Public Interest* 28: 38–50.

Easton, David. 1957. "An Approach to the Analysis of Political Systems." *World Politics* 9: 383–400.

Eavey, Cheryl L. and Gary J. Miller. 1984. "Bureaucratic Agenda Control: Imposition or Bargaining?" *American Political Science Review* 78, 3: 719–33.

Edelman, Murray. 1985. *The Symbolic Uses of Politics.* Chicago: University of Illinois Press.

Edwards, George C. III. 1989. *At the Margins: Presidential Leadership of Congress.* New Haven: Yale University Press.

Edwards, George C. III and Ira Sharkansky. 1978. *The Policy Predicament: Making and Implementing Public Policy.* San Francisco: W. H. Freeman and Company.

Edwards, George C. III and B. Dan Wood. 1999. "Who Influences Whom? The President, Congress, and the Media. *American Political Science Review* 93, 2: 327–44.

Epstein, David and Sharyn O'Halloran. 1996. "Divided Government and the Design of Administrative Procedures: A Formal Model and Empirical Test." *The Journal of Politics* 58, 2: 373–97.

———. 1994. "Administrative Procedures, Information, and Agency Discretion: Slack vs. Flexibility." *American Journal of Political Science* 38: 697–722.

Ethridge, Marcus E. 1984. "A Political-Institutional Interpretation of Legislative Oversight Mechanisms & Behavior." *Polity* 17, 2: 340–59.

Evans, Diana M. 1994. "Policy and Pork: The Use of Pork Barrel Projects to Build Policy Coalitions in the House of Representatives." *American Journal of Political Science* 38, 4: 894–917.

Faucheux, Ron. 1995. "The Grassroots Lobbying Explosion in the U.S." *Campaigns and Elections* 16, 1: 20–25.

Fenno, Richard F. 1997. *Learning to Govern.* Washington, DC: Brookings Institution Press.

———. 1973. *Congressmen in Committees.* Boston: Little, Brown.

———. 1966. *The Power of the Purse: Appropriations Politics in Congress.* Boston: Little, Brown.

Ferejohn, John A. 1986. "Logrolling in an Institutional Context: A Case Study of Food Stamp Legislation." In *Congress and Policy Change.* Eds. Gerald C. Wright, Jr., Leroy N. Rieselbach, and Lawrence C. Dodd. New York: Agathon.

———. 1974. *Pork Barrel Politics: Rivers and Harbors Legislation, 1947–1968.* Stanford, CA: Stanford University Press.

Fesler, James W. and Donald F. Kettle. 1996. *The Politics of the Administrative Process.* Chatham, NJ: Chatham House Publishers.

Finer, Herman. 1941. "Administrative Responsibility in Democratic Government." *Public Administration Review* 1 (Summer): 335–50.

Fiorina, Morris. 1977. *Congress: Keystone of the Washington Establishment.* New Haven: Yale University Press.

Fisher, Louis. 1983. "Annual Authorizations: Durable Roadblocks to Biennial Budgeting." *Public Budgeting & Finance* 3: 23–40.

———. 1979. "The Authorization-Appropriations Process in Congress: Formal Rules and Informal Practices." *Catholic University Law Review.*

———. 1975. *Presidential Spending Power.* Princeton: Princeton University Press.

Fleming, Roy B., B. Dan Wood, and John Bohte. 1999. "Attention to Issues in a System of Separated Powers: The Macrodynamics of America Policy Agendas." *Journal of Politics* 61, 1: 76–108.

Fox, Douglas M. and Charles H. Clapp. 1970. "The House Rules Committee's Agenda-Setting Function, 1961–1968." *Journal of Politics* 32, 2: 440–43.

Galloway, George B. 1951. "The Operation of the Legislative Reorganization Act of 1946." *The American Political Science Review* 45, 1: 41–68.

Gill, Jeff. 1999. "The Insignificance of Null Hypothesis Significance Testing." *Political Research Quarterly* 52, 3: 647–74.

Goodnow, Frank J. 1900. *Politics and Administration: A Study in Government.* New York: Russell & Russell.

Gordon, John Steele. 1997. *Hamilton's Blessing: The Extraordinary Life and Times of Our National Debt.* New York: Walker.

Greene, William H. 1997. *Econometric Analysis.* 3rd ed. Upper Saddle River, NJ: Prentice Hall.

Hall, Richard L. 1996. *Participation in Congress.* New Haven: Yale University Press.

Hall, Richard L. and Bernard Grofman. 1990. "The Committee Assignment Process and the Conditional Nature of Committee Bias." *The American Political Science Review* 84, 4: 1149–66.

Hall, Thad E. and Laurence J. O'Toole, Jr. 2004. "Shaping Formal Networks through the Regulatory Process." *Administration and Society* (forthcoming).

———. 2000. "Structures for Policy Implementation: An Analysis of National Legislation, 1965–1966 and 1993–1994." *Administration & Society* 31, 6: 667–86.

Hamilton, Alexander, James Madison, John Jay. 1961. *The Federalist Papers.* Edited by Clinton Rossiter. New York: NAL Penguin.

Hammond, Thomas H. 1986. "Agenda Control, Organizational Structure, and Bureaucratic Politics." *American Journal of Political Science* 30: 379–420.

Hansen, John Mark. 1991. *Gaining Access: Congress and the Farm Lobby, 1919–1981.* Chicago: University of Chicago Press.

———. 1985. "The Political Economy of Group Membership." *American Political Science Review* 79: 79–96.

Harbridge, Laurel. 2003. "Bill Introductions and Short-Term Authorizations." Senior Thesis, University of Colorado (conducted under the supervision of Scott Adler).

Havemann, Joel. 1978. *Congress and the Budget.* Bloomington: Indiana University Press.

Heinz, John P., Edward O. Laumann, Robert L. Nelson, and Robert H. Salisbury. 1993. *The Hollow Core: Private Interests in National Policy Making.* Cambridge, MA: Harvard University Press.

Henry, Nicholas. 1992. *Public Administration and Public Affairs.* Englewood Cliffs, NJ: Prentice Hall.

Ippolito, Dennis. 1981. *Congressional Spending: A Twentieth Century Report.* Ithaca, NY: Cornell University Press.

Jefferson, Thomas. 1977. *The Portable Thomas Jefferson.* Edited by Merrill D. Peterson. New York: Penguin Books.

Jenkins-Smith, Hank C., Gilbert K. St. Clair, and Brian Woods. 1991. "Explaining Change in Policy Subsystems: Analysis of Coalition Stability and Defection Over Time." *American Journal of Political Science* 35, 4: 851–80.

Jones, Bryan D., Frank R. Baumgartner, and Jeffrey C. Talbert. 1993. "The Destruction of Issue Monopolies in Congress." *American Political Science Review* 87, 3: 657–71.

Kennedy, Peter. 1998. *A Guide to Econometrics.* 4th ed. Cambridge, MA: MIT Press.

Kerwin, Cornelius M. 1999. *Rulemaking: How Government Agencies Write Law and Make Policy.* 2nd ed. Washington, DC: Congressional Quarterly Press.

Kiewiet, D. Roderick and Mathew D. McCubbins. 1991. *The Logic of Delegation: Congressional Parties and the Appropriations Process.* Chicago: University of Chicago Press.

King, David. 1997. *Turf Wars: How Congressional Committees Claim Jurisdiction.* Chicago: University of Chicago Press.

Kingdon, John W. 1995. *Agendas, Alternatives, and Public Policies.* New York: HarperCollins College Publishers.

Krehbiel, Keith. 1998. *Pivotal Politics: A Theory of U.S. Lawmaking.* Chicago: University of Chicago Press.

———. 1991. *Information and Legislative Organization.* Ann Arbor: University of Michigan Press.

———. 1990. "Are Congressional Committees Composed of Preference Outliers?" *The American Political Science Review* 84, 1: 149–63.

———. 1987. "Why Are Congressional Committees Powerful?" *American Political Science Review* 81: 929–35.

Lee, Frances E. 2003. "Geographic Politics in the U.S. House of Representatives: Coalition Building and Distribution of Benefits." *American Journal of Political Science* 47, 4: 714–28.

———. 1998. "Representation and Public Policy: The Consequences of Senate Apportionment for the Geographic Distribution of Federal Funds." *Journal of Politics* 60, 1: 34–62.

LeLoup, Lance T. 1980. *The Fiscal Congress.* Westport, CT: Greenview Press.

Light, Paul C. 1991. *The President's Agenda.* Baltimore: Johns Hopkins University Press.

Loomis, Burdette. 1994. *Time, Politics, and Policies: A Legislative Year.* Lawrence: University Press of Kansas.

Lynn, Laurence E., Jr., Carolyn J. Heinrich, and Carolyn J. Hill. 2001. *Improving Governance: A New Logic for Empirical Research.* Washington, DC: Georgetown University Press.

Mayhew, David. 1974. *Congress: The Electoral Connection.* New Haven: Yale University Press.

McCubbins, Mathew D. 1985. "The Legislative Design of Regulatory Structure." *American Journal of Political Science:* 721–48.

McCubbins, Mathew, Roger Noll, and Barry Weingast. 1989. "Structure and Process, Politics and Policy: Arrangements and the Political Control of Agencies." *Virginia Law Review,* 431–83.

———. 1987. "Administrative Procedures as Instruments of Political Control. *Journal of Law, Economics, & Organization:* 243–77.

McCubbins, Mathew and Thomas Schwartz. 1984. "Congressional Oversight Overlooked: Police Patrols Versus Fire Alarms." *American Journal of Political Science* 28: 165–79.

McGuire, Kevin T. and Gregory A. Calderia. 1996. "Issues, Agendas, and Decision Making on the Supreme Court." *American Political Science Review* 90, 4: 853–65.

———. 1993. "Lawyers, Organized Interests, and the Law of Obscenity: Agenda Setting and the Supreme Court." *American Political Science Review,* 87, 3: 717–26.

Menard, Scott. 1995. *Applied Logistic Regression Analysis.* Thousand Oaks, CA: Sage Publications.

Meyers, Roy T. 1997. "Late Appropriations and Government Shutdowns: Frequency, Causes, Consequences, and Remedies." *Public Budgeting & Finance* 17: 25–38.

———. 1988. "Biennial Budgeting by the U.S. Congress." *Public Budgeting & Finance* 8: 21–32.

Milbank, Dana. 2002. "Karl Rove, Adding to His To-Do List." *Washington Post.* June 25: A-17.

Moe, Terry M. 1984. "The New Economics of Organization." *American Journal of Political Science* 78: 739–77.

Montjoy, Robert S. and Laurence J. O'Toole, Jr. 1979. "Toward a Theory of Policy Implementation: An Organizational Prospective." *Public Administration Review:* 465–76.

Mouw, Calvin J. and Michael B. MacKuen. 1992. "The Strategic Agenda in Legislative Politics." *American Political Science Review* 86, 1: 87–105.

Munger, Michael C. 1988. "Allocation of Desirable Committee Assignments: Extended Queues versus Committee Expansion." *American Journal of Political Science* 32, 2: 317–44.

Nakamura, Robert T. and Frank Smallwood. 1980. *The Politics of Policy Implementation.* New York: St. Martin's Press.

Niskanen, William A. 1971. *Bureaucracy and Representative Government.* Chicago: Aldine–Atherton.

Ogul, Morris S. 1976. *Congress Oversees the Bureaucracy.* Pittsburgh: University of Pittsburgh Press.

Ogul, Morris S. and Bert A. Rockman. 1990. "Overseeing Oversight: New Departures and Old Problems." *Legislative Studies Quarterly* XV, 1: 5–24.

Oleszek, Walter J. 1989. *Congressional Procedures and the Policy Process.* 3rd ed. Washington, DC: Congressional Quarterly, Inc.

Ostrom, Vincent. 1989. *The Intellectual Crisis in American Public Administration.* Tuscaloosa, AL: The University of Alabama Press.

O'Toole, Jr., Laurence J. and Thad E. Hall. N.D. "Agencies as Agents?: Units of Analysis for Exploring Oversight and Control." Unpublished manuscript.

Pressman, Jeffrey L. and Aaron Wildavsky. 1984. *Implementation: How Great Expectations in Washington Are Dashed in Oakland: Or, Why It's Amazing That Federal Programs Work at All, This Being a Saga of the Economic Development Administration as Told by Two Sympathetic Observers Who Seek to Build Morals on a Foundation of Ruined Hopes.* 3rd ed. Berkeley: University of California Press.

Rochefort, David and Roger Cobb. 1994. *The Politics of Problem Definition: Shaping the Policy Agenda.* Lawrence: University of Kansas Press.

Rockman, Bert A. 1984. "Legislative-Executive Relations and Legislative Oversight." *Legislative Studies Quarterly* IX, 3: 387–440.

Rogers, James R. 1998. "Bicameral Sequence: Theory and State Legislative Evidence." *American Journal of Political Science* 42, 4: 1025–60.

Rosenbloom, David H. 2000. *Building a Legislative-Centered Public Administration: Congress and the Administrative State, 1946–1999.* Tuscaloosa: University of Alabama Press.

Sabatier, Paul A. and Hank C. Jenkins-Smith. 1999. "The Advocacy Coalition Framework: An Assessment." In *Theories of the Policy Process.* Ed. Paul Sabatier. Boulder, CO: Westview Press.

Sabatier, Paul A. and Hank C. Jenkins-Smith (Eds.). 1993. *Policy Change and Learning: An Advocacy Coalition Approach.* Boulder, CO: Westview Press.

Salisbury, Robert H. and Kenneth A. Shepsle. 1981. "Congressman as Enterprise." *Legislative Studies Quarterly* VI: 559–76.

Sayrs, Lois W. 1989. *Pooled Time Series Analysis.* Newbury Park, CA: Sage Publications.

Scher, Seymour. 1963. "Conditions for Legislative Control." *Journal of Politics* 25: 526–51.

Schick, Allen. 1995. *The Federal Budget: Politics, Policy, and Process.* Washington, DC: The Brookings Institution.

———. 1983. *Making Economic Policy in Congress.* Washington, DC: American Enterprise Institute for Public Policy Research.

———. 1980. *Congress and Money: Budgeting, Spending, and Taxing.* Washington, DC: The Urban Institute.

Schlozman, Kay Lehman and John T. Tierney. 1986. *Organized Interests and American Democracy.* New York: Harper & Row.

———. 1983. "More of the Same: Washington Pressure Group Activity in a Decade of Change." *The Journal of Politics* 45, 2: 351–77.

Shafritz, Jay M. and Albert C. Hyde. 1997. *Classics of Public Administration.* New York: Harcourt Brace College Publishers.

Shepsle, Kenneth A. 1978. *The Giant Jigsaw Puzzle: Democratic Committee Assignments in the Modern House.* Chicago: University of Chicago Press.

Shepsle, Kenneth A. and Mark S. Bonchek. 1997. *Analyzing Politics: Rationality, Behaviors, and Institutions.* New York: W.W. Norton.

Shepsle, Kenneth A. and Barry R. Weingast. 1987a. "The Institutional Foundation of Committee Power." *American Political Science Review* 81: 85–104.

———. 1987b. "Why Are Congressional Committees Powerful: Reply to Krehbiel." *American Political Science Review* 8, 1: 935–44.

Shuman, Howard E. 1992. *Politics and the Budget: The Struggle between the President and the Congress.* 3rd ed. Englewood Cliffs, NJ: Simon and Schuster.

Sinclair, Barbara. 1997. *Unorthodox Lawmaking: New Legislative Processes in the U.S. Congress.* Washington, DC: CQ Press.

———. 1995. *Legislators, Leaders, and Lawmaking: The U.S. House of Representatives in the Postreform Era.* Baltimore: Johns Hopkins University Press.

Skowronek, Stephen. 1993. *The Politics That Presidents Make.* Cambridge, MA: Belknap Press, 1993.

———. 1982. *Building a New American State: The Expansion of National Administrative Capacities, 1877–1920.* Cambridge: Cambridge University Press.

Skowronek, Stephen and Karen Orren. 1994. "Beyond the Iconography of Order: Notes for a 'New Institutionalism.'" In *The Dynamics of American Politics.* Eds. Lawrence Dodd and Calvin Jillson. Boulder, CO: Westview Press.

Smith, Steven S. and Christopher J. Deering. 1990. *Committees in Congress.* 2nd ed. Washington, DC: CQ Press.

Steinberg, Jacques. 2001. "Bush's Plan to Push Reading in 'Head Start' Stirs Debate." *The New York Times.* February 10: A-1.

Stewart, Charles H. 1989. *Budget Reform Politics: The Design of the Appropriations Process in the House of Representatives, 1986–1921.* Cambridge: Cambridge University Press.

Stienmo, Sven et al. (Eds.). 1992. *Structuring Politics: Historical Institutionalism in Comparative Analysis.* Cambridge: Cambridge University Press.

Stone, Deborah A. 1997. *Policy Paradox: The Art of Political Decision Making.* New York: W.W. Norton.

Stone, P. H. 1997. "Business Strikes Back." *National Journal* 29, 43: 2130–33.

Talbert, Jeffrey C., Bryan D. Jones, and Frank R. Baumgartner. 1995. "Nonlegislative Hearings and Policy Change in Congress." *American Journal of Political Science* 39, 2: 383–405.

Taylor, Andrew J. 2001. "Congress as Principal: Exploring Bicameral Differences in Agent Oversight." *Congress & the Presidency* 28, 2: 141–59.

Thurber, James A. 1997. "Congressional Budget Reform: Impact on the Appropriations Committees." *Public Budgeting & Finance* 17: 62–73.

Tiefer, Charles. 1989. *Congressional Practice and Procedure: A Reference, Research, and Legislative Guide.* New York: Greenwood Press.

True, James L., Bryan D. Jones, and Frank R. Baumgartner. 1999. "Punctuated-Equilibrum Theory: Explaining Stability and Change in American Policymaking." In *Theories of the Policy Process.* Ed. Paul Sabatier. Boulder, CO: Westview Press.

U.S. Code Congressional and Administrative News. 1965. "Public Law 89–4." *U.S. Code Congressional and Administrative News.* New York: West Group.

Wanat, John. 1978. *Introduction to Budgeting.* North Scituate, MA: Duxbury.

Weaver, R. Kent. 1988. *Automatic Government: The Politics of Indexation.* Washington, DC: Brookings Institution.

Weingast, Barry R. 1984. "The Congressional-Bureaucratic System: A Principal Agent Perspective (with application to the SEC). *Public Choice* 44: 147–91.

Weingast, Barry R. and William Marshall. 1988. "The Industrial Organization of Congress. *Journal of Political Economy* 96: 132–63.

White, Leonard D. 1951. *The Jeffersonians.* New York: Macmillan Company.

———. 1948. *The Federalists.* New York: Macmillan.

———. 1926. *Introduction to the Study of Public Administration.* Upper Saddle River, NJ: Prentice Hall.

Wildavsky, Aaron. 1992. *The New Politics of the Budgetary Process.* 2nd ed. New York: Longman.

Wildavsky, Aaron and Naomi Caiden.1997. *The New Politics of the Budgetary Process, 1997.* 3rd ed. New York: Longman.

Wilson, James Q. 1989. *Bureaucracy: What Government Agencies Do and Why They Do It.* New York: Basic Books.

Wilson, Woodrow. 1887. "The Study of Administration." *Political Science Quarterly* 2.

Wood, Dan B. and Jeffrey S. Peake. 1998. "The Dynamics of Foreign Policy Agenda Setting." *American Political Science Review* 92, 1: 173–84.

Wright, John R. 1996. *Interest Groups & Congress: Lobbying, Contributions, and Influence.* Boston: Allyn and Bacon.

Index of Names

Index of Subjects

PARLIAMENTS AND LEGISLATURES
Janet M. Box-Steffensmeier and David T. Canon, Series Editors

Citizens as Legislators: Direct Democracy in the United States
Shaun Bowler, Todd Donovan, and Caroline J. Tolbert, eds.

Party Discipline and Parliamentary Government
Shaun Bowler, David M. Farrell, and Richard S. Katz, eds.

Cheap Seats: The Democratic Party's Advantage in U.S. House Elections
James E. Campbell

Coalition Government, Subnational Style:
Multiparty Politics in Europe's Regional Parliaments
William M. Downs

Beyond Westminster and Congress: The Nordic Experience
Peter Esaiasson and Knut Heidar, eds.

Authorizing Policy
Thad Hall

Parliamentary Representation: The Case of the Norwegian Storting
Donald R. Matthews and Henry Valen

Creating Parliamentary Government:
The Transition to Democracy in Bulgaria
Albert P. Melone

Comparing Post-Soviet Legislatures: A Theory of Institutional Design and
Political Conflict
Joel M. Ostrow

Senates: Bicameralism in the Contemporary World
Samuel C. Patterson and Anthony Mughan, eds.

Politics, Parties, and Parliaments: Political Change in Norway
William R. Shaffer

Hitching a Ride: Omnibus Legislation in the U.S. Congress
Glen S. Krutz

Committees in Post-Communist Democratic Parliaments: Comparative Institutionalization
David M. Olson and William E. Crowther, eds.

U.S. Senate Exceptionalism
Bruce I. Oppenheimer, ed.

Reforming Parliamentary Committees: Israel in Comparative Perspective
Reuven Y. Hazan

Political Consultants in U.S. Congressional Elections
Stephen K. Medvic

Congress Responds to the Twentieth Century
Sunil Ahuja and Robert E. Dewhirst, eds.